The Instant Guide to Healthy
Foliage
Houseplants

Series editor: David Longman

Colour illustrations by Andrew Riley

The Instant Guide to Healthy
Foliage Houseplants

David Longman

Times
BOOKS

THE AUTHOR
David Longman is an expert in plant care who trained at the Royal
Horticultural Society's school at Wisley before joining his long-
established family firm of florists. A past Master of the Worshipful
Company of Gardeners, he is a council member of Interflora, a
director of the Flower and Plant Council and a regular exhibitor at
the Chelsea Flower Show. He is General Editor of this series.

Originally published in Great Britain in 1983 as *How to Care for
Your Foliage Houseplants* by Peter Lowe, London.

Library of Congress Catalog Card Number: 84-40634
International Standard Book Number: 0-8129-1173-3

Printed in Italy by Amilcare Pizzi SpA

987654321
First American Edition

Contents

6 Introduction, How to use this book
7 Tools for indoor gardening
8 Watering, Cleaning, Humidity, Feeding, Pruning
10 Choosing compost, Repotting, Propagation
12 Climbing plants, Using insecticides

Common names

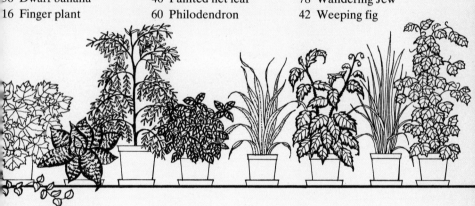

Scientific names

Introduction

How to use this book

Houseplants have now become so much part of everyday life that they are available at many types of shops from garden centres to motorway service stations. With the wide range of plants on sale, it is easy to make expensive mistakes. Despite the brief instruction labels provided with most purchases, a plant that has taken a nurseryman years to grow can be destroyed in a matter of weeks by either wrong treatment or from being in the wrong position. This book, one of two volumes on foliage plants in a comprehensive houseplant series, is here to help you.

Foliage houseplants are those grown for the beauty of their leaves rather than for their flowers. Here each one is given a self-contained two-page entry. On the left is a general description of the plant with details of how to look after it, giving the correct amounts of water, light, warmth and humidity it needs, explaining how to clean and repot it and when and if it needs pruning. There is also a colour photo of a healthy leaf. On the right-hand page is a colour illustration of the plant showing all the things that can go wrong with it. Since this picture shows all the troubles at once, some of the plants look very sick indeed! To find out what is wrong with your plant, look for its symptoms on the illustration. Read the caption next to the part of the picture that shows the same features as your plant. It tells you what is wrong and how to put it right.

Different plants require different care and conditions, so whether you are beginning with a familiar climbing Ivy or progressing to a more difficult species like a Prayer plant *(Calathea),* make sure you read the detailed care instructions for your plant and you will be able to look after it with confidence.

Tools for indoor gardening

It is possible to look after plants with the minimum of equipment: a watering can, sprayer and plastic sponge are the real essentials. However, for long-term houseplant care, you will need a much more comprehensive collection, which can be acquired gradually as the need arises.

Keep separate sprayers and watering cans for insecticides and fungicides and a stock of basic insecticides. Methylated spirits is useful for removing some pests. Mark all containers used for insecticides clearly and wash them out regularly.

Leafshine adds gloss but some plants react badly. These should be cleaned with a damp sponge or soft cloth, or with a fine mist spray. For delicate leaves use a feather duster or dry paintbrush. A paintbrush and cotton wool are useful for removing pests.

A small garden trowel and fork are useful when repotting or adding topsoil. A large spoon is a good substitute. A plastic bucket is essential for mixing composts, wetting peat and for giving very dry olants a thorough soaking.

Keep a selection of loam-based and peat-based composts, some pure moss or sedge peat. Some plants require lime-free mixtures. Sharp sand can be obtained from garden centres. Fertilizer, hormone rooting powder and charcoal are all useful.

Scissors, secateurs and a sharp knife are useful for removing dead or damaged fronds.

Two watering cans to which a rose can be attached are useful, one pint (½ litre) size, the other holding about a gallon (4½l). Never use your normal watering can for insecticides or fungicides. .

Keep a small stock of flower pots and saucers, both plastic and clay. Old clay flower pots can be broken up to make excellent drainage material. Outer pots, with no drainage holes, can be used to hide the standard pot.

Twine, string, raffia and plant rings are essential for climbing plants, with a selection of canes, sticks and moss poles.

Watering and spraying

More houseplants are killed by incorrect watering (mainly of the little and often variety) than by anything else. Most prefer to be given a good soaking, then left almost to dry out before they are watered again. Some must be kept always moist – but in these cases the pot must be well drained so that the roots do not become waterlogged. Others prefer to dry out more thoroughly between waterings. Some need more water at one time of year than another. Always test the compost before watering to see how dry it is below the surface. In cold weather do not use cold water straight from the tap or the shock may damage the plant. Use tepid water for both watering and spraying.

Spraying keeps a plant's leaves clean and also provides extra humidity in hot, dry rooms. Avoid tap water if possible as the lime it contains clogs the pores of the leaves. Rainwater collected in a tank or bucket, water from melted ice in the freezer or boiled water which has been allowed to cool are all more suitable. Do not spray in bright sunlight as the water acts like a magnifying glass and may cause burn or scorch marks. A few plants dislike water on their leaves so before spraying you should check the individual requirements under each plant entry. Most, however benefit from a fine mist spray.

Feeding

Most composts contain fertilizer but for healthy growth plants also need extra nourishment, usually in spring and summer. Houseplant food or fertilizer is available as a liquid, diluted before use, as a powder added to water, as granules scattered on the surface of the soil and as a pill or stick pushed into the soil and gradually absorbed. You can also obtain a foliar feed which is sprayed onto the leaves. For most houseplants a liquid food is most suitable. It is clean, has no smell, and is easy and economical to use. There are several brands available and it is a good idea to try several and to change from time to time. Normally you

Watering

1. Test compost for dryness with finger or knife blade before watering. If blade comes out clean or soil dry and crumbly, compost is drying out. If soil sticks, it is still moist. Check instructions for each plant: some like a dry interval, others must be always moist.

2. Add water to top of compost, filling pot to the brim. Excess water will drain into saucer. After 15 minutes empty any water remaining in the saucer. Do not allow pot to stand in water.

3. If plant is very dried out and does not mind water on its leaves, plunge pot into bowl so that water covers pot rim. Spray leaves. Leave for 15 minutes, then take it out and allow it to drain.

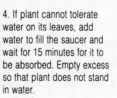

4. If plant cannot tolerate water on its leaves, add water to fill the saucer and wait for 15 minutes for it to be absorbed. Empty excess so that plant does not stand in water.

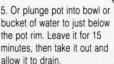

5. Or plunge pot into bowl or bucket of water to just below the pot rim. Leave it for 15 minutes, then take it out and allow it to drain.

Cleaning the leaves
1. Flick very dusty plants with a feather duster before cleaning.

2. Wipe larger leaves with a damp cloth to remove dust and any insects such as red spider mite. Use soft water if possible. Remember to wipe the undersides of the leaves as well as the tops.

3. Spraying (with soft water if possible) is often enough to keep plants clean. The lime in hard water may mark the leaves and clog the pores. Do not spray in sunlight.

4. Leafshine used not more than once a month (not more than once every 2 months in some cases) brings a glossy shine to the leaves. Check instructions for your plant as some can be damaged by leafshine.

Humidity
Some foliage plants require higher humidity than is found in normal rooms, especially in dry, centrally heated homes. A group of plants will create its own more humid atmosphere but you can improve the humidity around them in several ways.

1. Spray regularly with soft water, holding spray about 6in (15cm) from plant. Do not spray in strong sunlight. Spray may mark or rot flowers, so check plant's requirements when in flower.

2. Put pebbles in plant's saucer and stand pot on top. Add water to saucer until it comes half way up the pebbles. Do not let bottom of pot touch water or plant will become waterlogged and roots will rot away. Water vapour will rise from the damp pebbles, providing extra humidity under the leaves. Add more water to saucer when pebbles begin to dry. A group of plants can be placed together on a tray of damp pebbles for even better local humidity.

3. Place pot inside a larger container and pack the space between the two with damp peat. Keep peat constantly moist. This is a good method to use if you have to leave the plants for some time as the peat will hold moisture well.

Pruning

Old plants may grow straggly and woody. Pruning back leggy stems in spring encourages new side shoots which give a more bushy, compact appearance. In general, cut stems down by half, just above a leaf or side shoot. But read individual instructions as some must never be pruned.

Old dead leaves should be cut off as close to the stem as possible. This encourages new young leaves to develop.

can simply follow the instructions on the bottle, adding a few drops to the water in the can when watering. For some plants, however, the mixture must be weaker than the manufacturer recommends on the bottle. If it is used at too concentrated a strength, it will damage the roots. Never increase the recommended strength and be careful with tablets and fertilizer sticks. If they are too close to the roots, the concentrated fertilizer may cause root damage.

If in doubt, don't feed. It is always better to slightly underfeed than to overfeed – and never feed a sick plant.

Repotting

Plants need repotting either because the roots have totally filled the existing pot and can no longer develop or because the nutritional value of the compost has been used up. It's quite easy to tell if a plant needs repotting. Remove it from its pot (see right). If there is a mass of roots and no soil showing, it needs repotting – it is pot-bound. If any soil is visible, don't repot. Replace plant in its old pot and gently firm it back in position. Other signs are roots growing through the pot base and weak, slow growth. Newly purchased plants should not normally need repotting. Do not repot unhealthy plants: the shock may kill them. In fact if in doubt, don't repot.

Repotting is usually done in spring – March or April in the northern hemisphere, September or October in the southern. Most plants require good drainage so that water can run through the compost freely and air can get to its roots. Broken crocks from old clay flower pots or a layer of coarse gravel at the bottom of the pot will provide drainage. Never use a container without drainage holes in its base. Put a piece of paper or a layer of moss over the drainage crocks to stop the compost from blocking the holes and inspect the root ball for pests. Remove old stones, damaged roots and old soil and gently remove old, loose compost from the top to a depth of about ½in (1cm). Then place plant in new pot.

After repotting, leave the plant without water for 2–3 days. The roots will spread out into the new compost in search of water. If it is very hot, spray the leaves every day.

Choosing the right compost: The correct type of compost or soil is very important for indoor plants. Don't use ordinary soil, which is usually too heavy and stifles the roots of young plants. Compost types vary considerably as some houseplants need a very light peat-based compost and some a heavy loam. The correct combination for each plant is given in the individual entries.

The two most commonly used types of compost are loam-based or peat-based. Loam-based compost is made up of sterilized loam (soil) mixed with peat and grit or coarse, washed sand. It is usually sold with fertilizer added, following formulae developed by the John Innes Institute for Horticultural Research. The numbers 1, 2 and 3 indicate the different proportions of fertilizer added. In this book they are referred to as 'loam-based No. 1, 2 or 3'.

Peat-based composts are more open in

Division

1. A many-stemmed plant that has grown bushy can often be divided into 2, 3 or even 4 new plants. First water plant and prepare as many smaller pots as you need – see Repotting.

3. Gently pull roots and stems apart with your hands. For a very pot-bound plant with mass of roots, use a sharp knife. Make sure all sections have portion of root and stem.

2. Remove plant from pot and shake away loose soil from around the root ball. Remove bits of gravel or stones.

4. Repot the divided sections into the new pots. Leave in shade, without water, for 2–3 days so that roots will grow into compost.

Taking cuttings

This is the most common way of propagating houseplants though seeds of some species are available.

First prepare a small pot with drainage and special rooting compost.

3. Dust the cut ends with hormone rooting powder.

5. Place in heated propagator or cover with polythene and keep in warm place (70°F, 21°C). Keep watered and remove cover for 5 minutes a day.

1. Choose a healthy stem tip or side stem and cut off the top 3–4in (8–10cm). Cuttings should include a growing tip and 2 pairs of healthy leaves.

2. Remove lowest pair of leaves and any side shoots from bottom part so there is a length of bare stem to insert into compost. Prepare other cuttings in the same way.

4. Make holes around edge of new pot. Insert several cuttings and firm compost gently round them. Water well.

6. When cuttings begin to grow (in about 4 weeks), pot singly in small pots.

Layering

1. Some climbing or trailing plants can be layered. First prepare small pot with drainage and compost of half loam, half sharp sand.

Repotting

1. Prepare clean, dry pot not more than 2 sizes larger than old one. Place broken crocks or coarse gravel in bottom as drainage, then a piece of paper or moss and layer of new compost. Water plant well.

3. Remove damaged or dead roots with sharp knife.

5. Lower plant into new pot and add more compost round root ball, firming it with fingers or a round stick. Continue adding compost until pot is filled to within ½–¾in (1–1½cm). Leave without water in shade for 3 days.

2. Choose strong stem and make slit in lower surface, below a leaf.

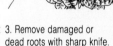

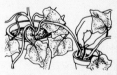

2. Hold pot upside down as shown. Gently tap rim of pot on edge of table and remove pot with other hand. If pot sticks, tap in several places.

4. Gently break roots at bottom of ball and remove any bits of crock or stone. Remove all loose, old compost from top, to a depth of about ½in (1cm). Always handle with care so as not to damage leaves or buds.

6. For large plants in tubs carefully scrape away about 2–3in (5–7cm) old topsoil. Add new compost, leaving ½–¾in (1–1½cm) space between compost and pot rim. Firm down well and water, including feed.

3. Bend stem so that slit stem lies on compost in new pot. Weight with pebble or peg closely to compost. Water. Roots will grow from slit and when these are firmly fixed, cut stem from parent plant with sharp knife.

Climbing plants

Some foliage plants are climbers and need to be trained up a cane or moss pole. Others need the support of a strong cane to keep their stems upright.

Canes

1. A single cane will support a tall plant or climber. Insert cane when repotting, after positioning plant but before adding all the compost. Cane should be a few inches from main stem, stopping about ⅔ down pot. If adding a cane at any other time, be careful not to damage roots as you push it in.

How to make a moss pole

Larger plants are best trained on a moss or foam pole. These retain moisture and any aerial roots will grow into the moss.

3. Bind moss along cane with string, tying off at top with a firm knot.

1. Choose a piece of strong cane long enough to reach top of plant from base of pot. Tie a piece of string to it, about 9in (22cm) from end.

4. Push uncovered end of cane into compost when repotting. If at any other time, be careful not to damage roots.

2. Take some sphagnum moss large enough to cover rest of cane and loosen it a little with a stick or pencil.

5. Tie plant loosely to moss pole in several places. Keep moss moist at all times. This helps humidity around plant.

---

texture, sterile, and hold moisture longer. They are normally composed of 10 parts of peat to 1 part of coarse sand with fertilizer added in the same proportions as loam-based compost. It is important when using peat composts not to firm them into the pot too hard.

Ericaceous or lime-free compost is available for plants that do not tolerate lime. Sphagnum moss is useful for some plants which are grown on cork bark or for lining a hanging basket. Sharp sand is fine, washed sand, available from garden centres. Do not use coarse builders' sand. It is sometimes mixed with loam to give a specially well-drained compost. Other useful items are small polystyrene balls to lighten the soil texture, rotted leafmould and manure.

Mixing compost: If mixing your own blend of compost, put the different items into a plastic bucket, using the same measure for each one. A plant pot or old cup will do. For 2 parts loam, 1 part peat, for example, fill the measure twice with loam, then once with peat. Mix the items together well with a trowel or stick so that they are well blended.

Insecticides

Unfortunately some houseplants are vulnerable to pests and diseases. The most common are mealy bug, scale insect, red spider mite and green or whitefly. These should be treated as soon as they are noticed and affected plants moved away from others to prevent the spread of infection. Plants with thin, delicate leaves, are attacked by insects such as red spider mite while greenfly are attracted to young leaves and stems. Some pests, such as mealy bug, appear on the leaves but may be carried hidden in the soil.

Insecticides are available usually as concentrated liquids which are added to water and sprayed or watered onto the infected plant, and as aerosols ready for use. Less usually, some chemicals for houseplants come in powdered form. This is not suitable for all plants – check the individual instructions. Systemic insecticides are absorbed into the plant's veins (its system) and so spread the poison to any insect which tries to take nourishment from these.

The least toxic insecticides are those based on pyrethrum and derris as these are both natural substances. They are most suited to whitefly and greenfly control. Derris is also suitable for whitefly and greenfly and controls red spider mite in the early stages. Methylated spirits can be used to remove scale insect and mealy bugs. Red spider can be prevented from recurring by improving humidity. Malathion is one of the most effective general insecticides and will control everything from whitefly to beetles, and especially mealy bug which is one of the most infectious and damaging insects likely to affect houseplants. Other insects such as scale insect and thrips can also be controlled by spraying malathion. It can be sprayed when diluted and also watered into the soil if the soil is infected.

Malathion may damage some sensitive plants, so read the captions carefully to make sure you choose the right treatment for your plant.

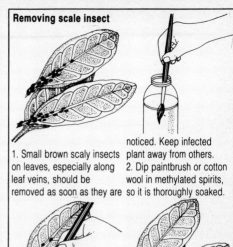

Removing scale insect

1. Small brown scaly insects on leaves, especially along leaf veins, should be removed as soon as they are noticed. Keep infected plant away from others.

2. Dip paintbrush or cotton wool in methylated spirits, so it is thoroughly soaked.

3. Dab each scale insect with methylated spirits to loosen it.

4. Remove with thumbnail. Make sure all insects are removed.

Taking care with insecticides

Insecticides and fungicides may contain deadly chemicals. Use them with care.

Never mix different types of insecticides as the chemicals may react.

Never put them into other bottles, such as soft drink or beer bottles.

Never breathe in the spray.

Never spray in windy weather.

Never pour them down the sink or drains. Do not even pour the water in which you have washed containers and sprayers down the drain.

Never make up more at one time than you will use.

Never keep diluted insecticide for more than 24 hours.

Never leave old containers lying around.

Always follow instructions carefully. Do not over or under dilute.

Always use a separate watering can and sprayer, keeping another one for normal spraying and watering.

Always keep away from food, crockery, glasses, food containers, and minerals. Derris is harmful to fish; malathion harms bees.

Always cover fish bowls when spraying.

Always store them with their sprayers and containers in a dry, frost free place, on a high shelf out of reach of children.

Always spray outside, in the evening when bees are not around.

Always wash out all sprayers and empty bottles after use, inside and out.

Always pour washing water onto ground away from food crops and water sources such as streams and rivers.

Always throw empty bottles and containers away with domestic waste.

Always wash thoroughly in hot water and detergent when you have used them.

Aglaonema treubii

Chinese evergreen

A much under-rated plant for growing in the house, Chinese evergreen will live in quite difficult conditions for plants and survive away from direct light and in dry situations. It is not a large plant and, in fact, looks better when kept on the small side. The spear-shaped leaves, which droop gracefully, are about 5–6in (12–15cm) long and will deteriorate only if the plant is underfed or is too cold in winter. If grown with other plants in a bowl or jardinière, its leaf shape makes a good contrast with that of other houseplants. It is suitable for hydroculture.

The easiest way to propagate these plants is by dividing young shoots in spring. Make sure each section has a good portion of roots and keep them warm (70°F, 21°C) until they are growing well.

The variety 'Silver Queen' with its pointed green leaves overlaid with silver, is the best known. It sometimes produces a small yellow or white flower, followed by red berries. Leaves should be firm and bright, with no sign of yellowing. It is a very suitable plant for hydroculture.

Light: North-facing light best, but will tolerate most conditions.
Temperature: prefers 60°F (15°C) in winter but will survive down to 50°F (10°C) if kept dry. Summer maximum 75°F (24°C).
Water: Twice a week in summer, not more than once a week in winter, and less if very cold. Water from top, allowing surplus to drain away. Do not stand in water.
Humidity: Spray twice a week in summer, but not in direct sunshine. Do not spray in winter.
Feeding: Every 14 days in the growing season (spring and summer) with house-plant food diluted according to the maker's instructions.
Soil: Loam-based No. 2 compost.
Repotting: Annually in spring. Likes open compost, so do not firm it down too hard in the pot.
Cleaning: By hand with damp cloth or with fine mist spray in summer. No leafshine.

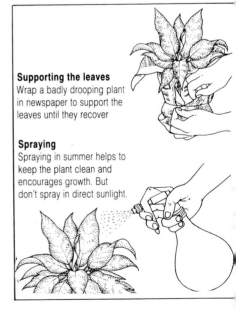

Supporting the leaves
Wrap a badly drooping plant in newspaper to support the leaves until they recover

Spraying
Spraying in summer helps to keep the plant clean and encourages growth. But don't spray in direct sunlight.

what goes wrong

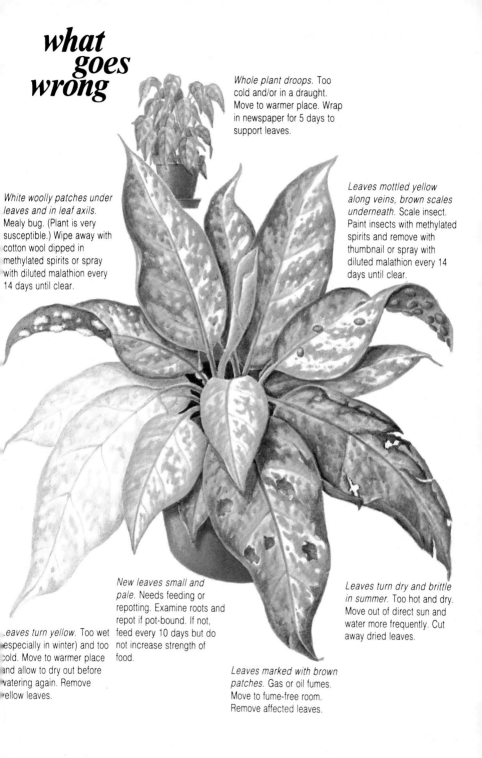

Whole plant droops. Too cold and/or in a draught. Move to warmer place. Wrap in newspaper for 5 days to support leaves.

White woolly patches under leaves and in leaf axils. Mealy bug. (Plant is very susceptible.) Wipe away with cotton wool dipped in methylated spirits or spray with diluted malathion every 14 days until clear.

Leaves mottled yellow along veins, brown scales underneath. Scale insect. Paint insects with methylated spirits and remove with thumbnail or spray with diluted malathion every 14 days until clear.

New leaves small and pale. Needs feeding or repotting. Examine roots and repot if pot-bound. If not, feed every 10 days but do not increase strength of food.

.eaves turn yellow. Too wet (especially in winter) and too cold. Move to warmer place and allow to dry out before watering again. Remove yellow leaves.

Leaves marked with brown patches. Gas or oil fumes. Move to fume-free room. Remove affected leaves.

Leaves turn dry and brittle in summer. Too hot and dry. Move out of direct sun and water more frequently. Cut away dried leaves.

Aralia elegantissima

Finger plant

As its name implies, this is a very elegant plant, with long, narrow, bronze leaves growing to 7–8in (18–20cm) long. It is also botanically interesting, as a single plant may carry three types of leaf: small baby leaves (cotyledons) at the base, juvenile leaves which are very pointed and, at the top, adult leaves which are flatter and wider. As a young plant, it is a good mixer in bowls as it makes a fine contrast in shape and colour with other plants. As it gets older, it makes a good specimen, growing into a tall tree-like plant. It flourishes in a good light, warm position, though it does not flower when grown as a houseplant. It can be grown quite easily from seed if kept around 70°F (21°C) or from stem-tip cuttings. These should also be kept warm and humid as they begin to root.

It is sometimes known by the scientific name *Dizygotheca* or False Aralia.

Light: Good light position away from direct sunlight.
Temperature: Winter minimum 60°F (15°C), summer maximum 70°F (21°C).
Water: Twice weekly in summer, once a week in winter, keeping moist at all times. Allow surplus to drain away. Soil must not dry out.
Humidity: Spray daily with mister, if possible, especially in summer heat.
Feeding: Every 14 days in the growing season (spring and summer) with houseplant food diluted according to the maker's instructions.
Soil: Loam-based No. 2 compost.
Repotting: Annually in spring, though plant prefers small pot.
Cleaning: Humidity misting sufficient. No leafshine.

Most Finger plants are sold while still producing only their elegantly pointed juvenile leaves. Later, their long bronze-coloured adult leaves may grow to 7–8in (18–20cm) long. Look for plants with bright leaves and branches growing all down the main stem.

Humidity
Spray daily with fine mist spray especially when temperature is near summer maximum 70°F, (21°C).

For extra local humidity, stand pot on saucer of pebbles almost covered with water. Don't let the pot base touch the water or roots will be waterlogged.

Bottom leaves drop without warning. Too dark; larger top leaves may be shading lower ones. Move to lighter place, but not full sun.

what goes wrong

Scorch marks on edges of leaves. Plant in direct sunlight. Move to light position but out of direct sun.

Plant grows slowly and new leaves are small. Needs feeding. Feed every 14 days in spring and summer.

White woolly patches on leaves and stems. Mealy bug. Wipe with cotton wool dipped in methylated spirits or spray every 14 days with diluted malathion until clear.

Upper leaves drop off when still green. Too cold. Move to warmer position, at least 60° (15°C) in winter.

Leaf surfaces sticky with brown scales underneath. Scale insect. Wipe with cotton wool dipped in methylated spirits or spray every 14 days until clear with diluted malathion-based insecticide.

Leaves sticky, twisted and distorted, with small green insects. Greenfly. Spray every 14 days until clear with pyrethrum or a systemic insecticide.

Leaves go limp and droop. Plant waterlogged from overwatering. Allow to dry out before watering again, do not stand in water and check that drainage holes in pot are clear.

Leaves go dry and brittle, then drop off. Too hot and dry. Move to cooler place, spray with water more often. Water soil regularly.

17

Norfolk Island pine

This slow-growing plant is the only evergreen conifer suitable for growing in the home. Although its horizontal branches carrying soft needles seem almost oriental, it in fact comes from Norfolk Island off Australia in the south Pacific, hence its name. A very good specimen plant, it prefers to grow on its own. In its natural habitat, it grows to considerable heights, but in the home seldom reaches more than 60in (150cm). It likes plenty of air and not too high temperatures. It is related to the Monkey Puzzle tree *(A. araucana)* from Chile.

Norfolk Island pines grow very slowly, producing only one or sometimes two layers of new branches a year. The branches grow at distinct intervals on the main trunk and are covered with soft, attractive needles. These should at all times look fresh and bright: avoid plants with dried needles or stems.

Light: Keep out of direct sunlight in summer. Will tolerate shade, though prefers being near a window. Make sure that you turn the plant regularly, about once a week in spring and summer. Otherwise it will lean towards the light and lose its even shape.

Temperature: Winter minimum 40°F (5°C), summer maximum 60°F (16°C) if possible. Can be kept out-of-doors in summer.

Water: Twice weekly in summer, about every 7–10 days in winter, to keep soil just damp. Use soft water if possible.

Humidity: Spray twice weekly in summer, weekly in winter if in a centrally heated room.

Feeding: Every 14 days in the growing season (spring and summer) with houseplant food diluted with water. Use half the amount of food recommended by the maker.

Soil: A rich compost such as loam-based No. 2.

Repotting: Annually in spring when young. When over 39in (1m) tall, just replace topsoil with fresh compost.

Cleaning: Humidity spraying sufficient. No leafshine.

Branches hang down limply. Too cold. Move to warmer place, at least 40°F (5°C).

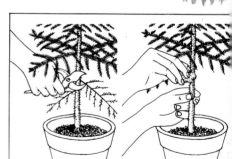

Pruning

1. Cut off bare branches cleanly close to main stem. Do not leave a jagged edge.

2. Dab cut with sulphur dust and if sap runs, use cotton wool dipped in vaseline to seal the cut ends.

what goes wrong

Plant does not grow. Needs repotting. Look at roots and if tightly packed, repot in pot one size larger.

White woolly patches on needles and spines. Mealy bug. If possible, remove with cotton wool dipped in methylated spirits. Or spray every 14 days with diluted malathion until clear.

Needles bleached. Too much sunlight through glass in summer. Move away from window into shadier place.

Branches grow thin and weedy, drooping under their own weight. Needs regular feeding. Increase strength of food to three-quarters maker's recommended strength.

Needles dry up and turn yellow and brown. Too hot and dry. Move to cooler, more airy room, water and spray regularly.

Green needles fall off. Overwatered. Allow to dry out before watering again, then water less often.

Needles sticky, with small green insects. Greenfly. Spray every 14 days with pyrethrum or a systemic insecticide until clear.

Needles drop from lower branches, leaving bare spines. In large plant, old age. Other plants may be in too dark a place. Move into lighter position and prune off dead branch close to main stem with sharp knife or secateurs.

19

Begonia

The foliage Begonias are most rewarding plants to grow for they have a wonderful variety of design and colour in each decorative leaf. They come originally from the Himalayas and are mostly used today in mixed plantings in bowls and troughs. Modern varieties owe much to nineteenth-century plant breeders, who produced the many types now available. One popular variety is *B. masoniana,* known as 'iron cross' from the brown cross pattern in the centre of its bright green leaves.

The beautifully shaped, pointed, slightly toothed leaves of foliage Begonias come in a great variety of delicate patterns in greens, reds, pinks and silvers. When buying, look for plants with crisp, unturned leaves without brown edges.

Light: Keep out of direct sunlight. Otherwise, keep as near to natural light as possible.

Temperature: Winter minimum 55°F (13°C), summer maximum 60–65°F (15–18°C).

Water: Twice weekly with soft water in summer, about every 10 days in winter to keep soil just moist. Water from the top but do not get water on leaves.

Humidity: Spray every 3–4 days with fine mist spray in summer. Stand pot on saucer on pebbles almost covered with water. If temperature drops, do not spray or stand on wet pebbles.

Feeding: Every 14 days in the growing season (spring and summer) with houseplant food diluted according to the maker's instructions.

Soil: Light, open mixture of peat-based compost or mixture of 2 parts loam, 2 parts peat, to 1 part leaf mould and 1 part sharp sand.

Repotting: Best in small pots, so repot only when roots very crowded, into next size pot. Take care not to damage leaves while handling.

Cleaning: Light feather dusting occasionally. No leafshine.

Leaves curl and go crisp at edges. Too hot and dry. Water well, avoiding crown at base of stem. Move to cooler place, below 65°F (18°C) if possible.

Leaves grow distorted and have yellow rings and mottling. Mosaic virus. Incurable. Burn plant to avoid infecting others.

Leaves drop in winter. Too cold. Move to warmer room, at least 55°F (13°C).

what goes wrong

White powdery patches spreading over leaves and stems. Powdery mildew. Spray once with benomyl-based fungicide and move plant to drier, more airy position.

Grey-brown powdery patches on leaves. Grey mould. Move to drier, more airy position and spray once with benomyl-based fungicide.

New leaves dull with fine webs underneath. Red spider mite. Spray every 14 days with derris, diluted malathion or a systemic insecticide until clear.

Leaves limp, plant droopy. Gas fumes. Move to fume-free room.

New leaves in spring stay small. Needs feeding or repotting. Examine roots and repot if they are crowded and growing through base of pot. Feed regularly.

Leaves become discoloured and then drop. Swellings on roots. Eel worm. No cure. Destroy plant.

Stem and crown rotting at base of plant. Too cold and too wet. Move to a warmer place and allow to dry out before watering again.

Roots black and rotting. Root rot, usually from overwatering. Spray roots with benomyl-based fungicide before repotting in fresh compost.

Prayer plant

This is not the easiest of houseplants to grow, though it is one of the most beautiful. The long, pointed leaves appear to be hand-painted, in delicate shades of green or green and brown. Its common name derives from the fact that the leaves resemble a Moslem prayer mat, or because indoors at night its leaves tend to curl like hands in prayer. Another variety of *Calathea, C. makoyana,* has slightly rounder, beautifully marked leaves. Both originate from South America. In summer, a small white flower grows on a stem but the plant's real beauty lies in its leaves. *Calatheas* are often confused with related and very similar *Marantas.* In general, *Calatheas* are the more upright plants.

The beautifully marked leaves of the Prayer plant grow on long 6in (15cm), stems from the centre of the plant. The upper surface has a very distinctive pattern which shows less clearly on the reddish underside. When buying, make sure that the leaves are clean, undamaged and with distinct colouring.

Leaves curl and close up. Natural at night. If they stay closed in the day, too cold. Move to warmer position, out of draughts.

Light: Prefers being out of direct light. Avoid sun-facing windows in summer.

Temperature: Winter minimum 60°F (16°C). Can take summer temperatures as high as 85°F (29°C), provided humidity is also high.

Water: 2–3 times a week in summer, once a week in winter. Never allow to dry out, though withhold water if temperature drops to 60°F (16°C).

Humidity: Mist daily in summer, twice a week in winter. Stand plant on saucer of pebbles almost covered with water. High humidity essential.

Feeding: Every 14 days when growing, with liquid houseplant food diluted with water. Use half as much food as the maker recommends.

Soil: Peat-based compost. Open, porous mix best.

Repotting: Annually in spring. If plants get too big for the space available, divide them.

Cleaning: If humidity spraying does not keep leaves clean, wipe with damp cloth.

Humidity
Calatheas need high humidity. Spray every day in summer, twice a week in winter.

To provide permanent local humidity, stand pot on saucer of pebbles. Add water to saucer, almost covering pebbles but don't let base of pot touch water.

what goes wrong

Leaves fade, lose colour and look slightly transparent with webs underneath. Red spider mite. Spray with derris, diluted malathion or systemic insecticide every 14 days until clear. Improve humidity.

Leaves turn pale. Too much direct sun. Move out of sun but keep in good light position.

Leaves curl and turn brown at edges. Too cold and dry. Move to warmer position (at least 60°F, 16°C) and water regularly. Remove damaged leaves by cutting stem close to soil level.

Leaves dull with white woolly patches at bases. Mealy bug. Remove with cotton wool dipped in methylated spirits or spray with diluted malathion every 14 days until clear.

Leaves droop, look dull and lifeless with brown, curling edges. Needs watering. Soak in bucket of water for 10–15 minutes, then drain. Keep moist always unless temperature less than 60°F (16°C).

Leaves droop limply. Too hot and dry. Soak in bucket of water for 10–15 minutes, then drain. Spray every day to improve humidity. Move to cooler place if possible.

Plant produces only small leaves which do not grow. Needs feeding. Feed every 14 days in spring and summer.

Japanese sedge plant

This is one of the few ornamental grasses that are worth cultivating as houseplants. A little stark on its own, it is seen to best advantage in mixed plantings, where its stiffness contrasts well with the round or oval leaves of many other houseplants. Its cream-striped leaves are very strong and upright, growing up to 12in (30cm) tall. They should be handled with care, since the leaf margins can cut badly. This plant is a fast grower and can be easily propagated by being divided into up to three parts in spring. It grows from an underground rhizome (a horizontal stem from which both shoots and roots are produced). Make sure each divided clump has a good portion of rhizome, root and stems and keep them moist and humid while they are becoming established.

The yellowish green leaves of the grass-like Japanese sedge plant have narrow white stripes, which disappear if the plant is not in a good light. Look for strong, upright leaves with no dried or withered ends.

Light: Likes good light position. Will stand full sun.
Temperature: Winter minimum 55°F (12°C), summer maximum 75°F (24°C).
Water: Up to 3 times a week in summer, once a week in winter, depending on temperature. Will wither if allowed to dry out.
Humidity: Mist at least twice weekly, as plant likes moist atmosphere.
Feeding: Every 14 days in growing season. Use liquid houseplant food diluted with water, using half as much food as the maker recommends.
Soil: Loam-based No. 2 compost.
Repotting: Annually in spring if plant is grown on its own. If in mixed bowl, divide plant when it gets out of balance with others in group.
Cleaning: Humidity spraying sufficient, though plant may be wiped with damp cloth if dirty.

Division
A plant that has outgrown its pot or is out of balance in a mixed planting can be divided in spring.

1. Remove from pot and gently tease stale soil from around rhizomes and roots.

2. Pull roots and stems apart carefully. Repot both sections. Do not divide into more than 3 sections.

what goes wrong

Leaves look dull and plant does not grow. Needs feeding. Feed regularly with half-strength houseplant food. Feed every 14 days in spring and summer.

Leaves shrivel and dry up. Too hot. Move to cooler position, and spray regularly.

Variegation disappears. Too dark. Move to lighter place.

Leaves grow lanky and lose stiffness. Overfeeding, either too often or with too strong a mixture. Do not feed until plant recovers.

Brown sticky patches towards base of leaves. Scale insect. Paint with methylated spirits or spray with diluted malathion every 14 days until clear.

Leaves wither, going thin and papery. Needs watering. Do not allow soil to dry out.

Leaves rot at base. Too wet, may be standing in water. Allow to dry out before watering again. This is rare.

Plant bursts over side of pot. Needs repotting and/or dividing. Do this in spring.

25

Spider plant

This is a wonderful plant for beginners as only determined neglect will kill it. It is a very quick grower. With its long, strap-like leaves coming from the centre of the plant, it is very good in hanging baskets as it throws out long stems which produce first small flowers and then plantlets. These hang down to make an attractive decoration. Young plants, which can easily be grown from the plantlets on the end of the stems, can be used for summer bedding out-of-doors. The plant, which originates from South Africa, grows well in hydroculture. It likes to be fed well, but also likes to be pot-bound. When its stems fill the pot and the white, worm-like rhizomes bulge out over the surface, it can easily be divided.

A Spider plant's long leaves grow from the centre of the plant and are usually green at the edges with a white stripe down the middle. Some varieties have white edges and a green central stripe. Look for clean, untorn leaves, with no brown tips.

Light: Grows in most positions, though its variation is most pronounced when plant is near a window. Keep away from mid-day sun.

Temperature: Very tolerant, though must be frost-free in winter.

Water: 2–3 times a week in summer, once a week in winter. Withhold water if temperature drops below 40°F (4°C).

Humidity: Spray daily in summer, twice a week in winter if temperature is over 60°F (15°C).

Feeding: Every 14 days in the growing season (spring and summer) with houseplant food diluted according to the maker's instructions.

Soil: Loam-based No. 2, to give roots a firm hold.

Repotting: About twice a year, though plant does not mind being pot-bound. It is all right to remove some of the fat white tubers or the rhizomes if they fill surface of pot.

Cleaning: Humidity spraying sufficient. No leafshine.

Separating the plantlets

1. Prepare small pots with drainage layer and compost.

2. Place new pot next to parent plant and bend stem until plantlet rests on compost. Peg stem to compost and firm soil around plantlet.

3. When plantlet grows new leaves, cut parent stem with sharp knife close to plantlet.

Leaves turn dark green and lose variegation. Too dark. Move to lighter place, in window out of direct sunlight.

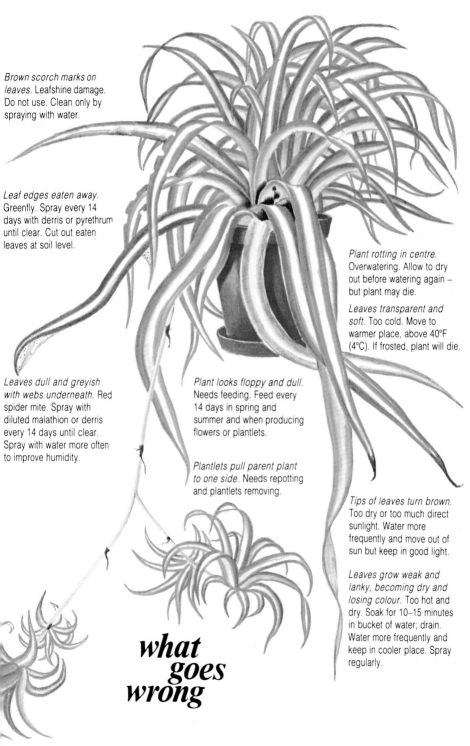

Brown scorch marks on leaves. Leafshine damage. Do not use. Clean only by spraying with water.

Leaf edges eaten away. Greenfly. Spray every 14 days with derris or pyrethrum until clear. Cut out eaten leaves at soil level.

Plant rotting in centre. Overwatering. Allow to dry out before watering again – but plant may die.

Leaves transparent and soft. Too cold. Move to warmer place, above 40°F (4°C). If frosted, plant will die.

Leaves dull and greyish with webs underneath. Red spider mite. Spray with diluted malathion or derris every 14 days until clear. Spray with water more often to improve humidity.

Plant looks floppy and dull. Needs feeding. Feed every 14 days in spring and summer and when producing flowers or plantlets.

Plantlets pull parent plant to one side. Needs repotting and plantlets removing.

Tips of leaves turn brown. Too dry or too much direct sunlight. Water more frequently and move out of sun but keep in good light.

Leaves grow weak and lanky, becoming dry and losing colour. Too hot and dry. Soak for 10–15 minutes in bucket of water; drain. Water more frequently and keep in cooler place. Spray regularly.

what goes wrong

27

Codiaeum variegatum

Croton

This is one of the most colourful of all houseplants, well deserving its other common name, Joseph's Coat. It needs plenty of light if it is to flourish. It is also difficult to overwinter in the house, so it is best regarded as a plant for one season only. When large, they are beautiful grown on their own, otherwise they are best in mixed bowls, where they benefit from the humidity provided by the other plants. The leaf shapes found on Crotons vary considerably, some being oval, some like large oak leaves and others narrow and strap-like. New leaves may be mainly green, developing their colours as they mature.

Though Croton leaf shapes vary, all are multicoloured, with strong yellow, red, or green markings and contrasting veins. New plants should have bright, glossy leaves growing right to the base of the stem.

Light: Needs plenty. Can be put in full sun, but if so should be sprayed in the middle of the day.

Temperature: Winter minimum 60°F (15°C), summer maximum 80°F (27°C). Prefers a steady temperature.

Water: 2–3 times a week in summer, every 4–5 days in winter, using tepid water. Never allow to dry out.

Humidity: Spray daily in summer, but not in direct sunlight. Spray weekly in winter. Stand on saucer of pebbles almost covered in water to help humidity. Don't allow pot base to touch water.

Feeding: Every 14 days in the growing season (spring and summer) with houseplant food diluted according to the maker's instructions.

Soil: Loam-based No. 2 compost.

Repotting: Annually in late spring, if plant has survived the winter. They prefer to be in a pot which is slightly too small.

Cleaning: By hand with damp cloth, or give a monthly spray of leafshine.

what goes wrong

Leaves shrivel. Too hot and too dry; air too dry. Water and spray more often. Move to cooler place if possible.

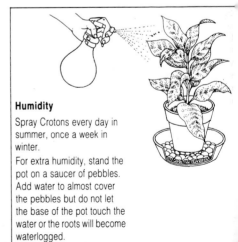

Humidity

Spray Crotons every day in summer, once a week in winter.

For extra humidity, stand the pot on a saucer of pebbles. Add water to almost cover the pebbles but do not let the base of the pot touch the water or the roots will become waterlogged.

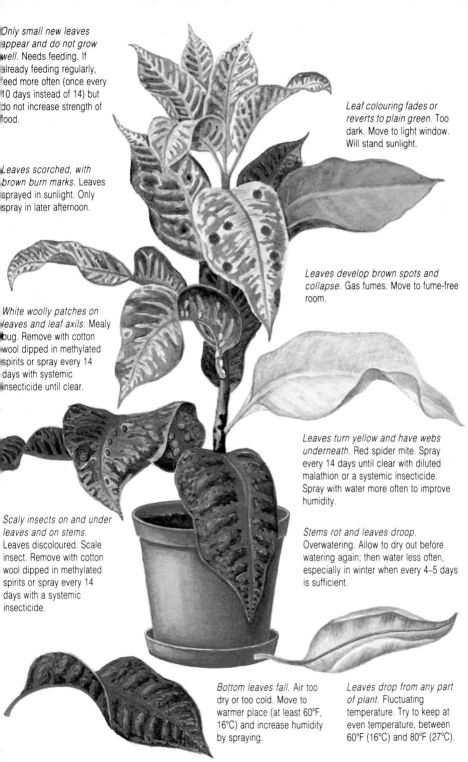

Only small new leaves appear and do not grow well. Needs feeding. If already feeding regularly, feed more often (once every 10 days instead of 14) but do not increase strength of food.

Leaf colouring fades or reverts to plain green. Too dark. Move to light window. Will stand sunlight.

Leaves scorched, with brown burn marks. Leaves sprayed in sunlight. Only spray in later afternoon.

Leaves develop brown spots and collapse. Gas fumes. Move to fume-free room.

White woolly patches on leaves and leaf axils. Mealy bug. Remove with cotton wool dipped in methylated spirits or spray every 14 days with systemic insecticide until clear.

Leaves turn yellow and have webs underneath. Red spider mite. Spray every 14 days until clear with diluted malathion or a systemic insecticide. Spray with water more often to improve humidity.

Scaly insects on and under leaves and on stems. Leaves discoloured. Scale insect. Remove with cotton wool dipped in methylated spirits or spray every 14 days with a systemic insecticide.

Stems rot and leaves droop. Overwatering. Allow to dry out before watering again; then water less often, especially in winter when every 4–5 days is sufficient.

Bottom leaves fall. Air too dry or too cold. Move to warmer place (at least 60°F, 16°C) and increase humidity by spraying.

Leaves drop from any part of plant. Fluctuating temperature. Try to keep at even temperature, between 60°F (16°C) and 80°F (27°C).

29

Coffee plant

Given the right conditions, it is almost possible to grow one's own coffee as well as drink it, for a *Coffea arabica* over three years old produces pretty little white, scented flowers which eventually produce cherry-like fruit which turn from green to red to black and so to coffee beans. The plant makes a handsome little shrub that does well in the house, for it enjoys semi-shade. Indoors it grows to about 4ft (just over 1m) tall, and there is a dwarf variety, *C. arabica* 'Nana'. It likes a good, airy position, but must not be in direct draughts.

Light: Does well in light windows that do not face the sun. Keep out of direct sunlight.

Temperature: Tolerates winter minimum of 45°F (8°C) if water withheld, but prefers 60°F (15°C). Normal room temperatures acceptable in summer.

Water: Up to 3 times a week in summer, depending on temperature. Do not let the compost dry out completely. Once a week is enough in winter. If temperature falls to 45°F (8°C) allow compost to dry out.

Humidity: Spray twice a week in summer, more often if over about 75°F (24°C). Spray every 14 days in winter with tepid water.

Feeding: Every 14 days in the growing season (spring and summer) with house-plant food diluted according to the maker's instructions.

Soil: Peat-based compost, with fertilizer at same strength as loam-based No. 2 (see p. 10).

Repotting: Annually in spring when plant starts to grow.

Cleaning: Humidity spraying sufficient. Use leafshine but not more than once a month.

The Coffee plant's leaves are oblong-oval, with a distinct point. When young they have a coppery tinge but soon turn a dark, glossy green, with a very shiny surface. If conditions are correct, the plant will flower – and produce a small crop of coffee beans.

Brown scorch marks on leaves. Caused by water left on leaves after spraying in sunlight. Spray in the evening.

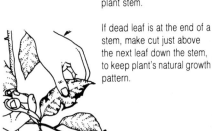

Removing damaged leaves
Cut off single discoloured or dead leaves with scissors at point where leaf stem joins plant stem.

If dead leaf is at the end of a stem, make cut just above the next leaf down the stem, to keep plant's natural growth pattern.

New leaves stay small. Needs repotting. If plant does not grow in spring, too cold. Move to warmer position, at least 60°F (15°C).

Leaves fall off while still green. Too dark. Move into lighter position, but not full sun.

Greyish white mildew on leaves and stems. Too wet. Allow to dry out before watering again and keep at a temperature of at least 60°F (15°C).

Edges of leaves burn. Too much sun from one direction. Move out of sunlight. If leaves are unsightly, cut them off where they join side stem.

Leaves dry up and turn brown. Too hot. Move to cooler place if possible; spray every day if temperature over about 75°F (24°C).

Leaves lose their shine. Too much light. Move out of direct sun.

White woolly patches on leaves and in stem axils. Mealy bug. Wipe with cotton wool dipped in methylated spirits or spray every 14 days with diluted malathion until clear.

what goes wrong

Leaves flop and collapse. Needs watering. Do not allow compost to dry out in summer.

Brown sticky patches under leaves. Scale insect. Wipe with cotton wool dipped in methylated spirits or spray every 14 days with diluted malathion until clear.

Leaves shrivel and fall. Air too dry. Spray daily when temperature over 75°F (24°C) and stand pot on pebbles not quite covered with water.

31

Starfish

One of the smallest plants in the family known as Bromeliads, the Starfish plant is a real sun lover, and the more light it gets the brighter is the colour on its flat leaves. The plant has a poor root system, which tethers it rather than giving nourishment, so it grows well in a little moss wired to a piece of log or bark. Thus it makes a good hanging decoration, though, with its striped leaves, it also looks attractive in the front of a bowl of mixed plants. Young plantlets are produced in the axils of the leaves and, unlike other Bromeliads, the mother plant does not die after producing them. Several species are available with differently patterned or coloured leaves.

The Starfish plant has leaves which grow to only about 4in (10cm) long. It grows well with other plants in bowls or bottle gardens and, because it has a small root system, can easily be grown attached to a piece of bark.

Light: The more the better. Do not allow water on the leaves in full sun, as it will scorch them.
Temperature: Winter range 60–65°F (15–18°C), summer maximum 75°F (24°C).
Water: 2–3 times a week in summer, especially if tied to moss. About every 10 days in winter. They do not need to have water in their central well, keeping the roots moist is sufficient.
Humidity: Spray every day in summer with fine mist when temperature is near maximum.
Feeding: Not essential, though a weak dose of houseplant food every 21 days in summer will help keep it in good condition. Dilute the food so that it is half the strength recommended by the makers.
Soil: Peaty compost mixed with a handful of sphagnum moss if in pots.
Repotting: Not required, as pot is really only a means of anchoring plant. Every 2 or 3 years is enough.
Cleaning: Spray or dust if dirty. No leaf-shine.

what goes wrong

Leaves shrivel and become thin and papery. Too hot and dry. Water more often, spray regularly and move to a cooler place if possible.

Leaves dull and droopy. Too dark. Move to lighter place. Can stand full sunlight.

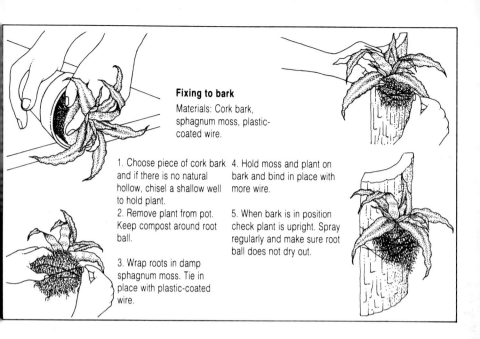

Fixing to bark

Materials: Cork bark, sphagnum moss, plastic-coated wire.

1. Choose piece of cork bark and if there is no natural hollow, chisel a shallow well to hold plant.

2. Remove plant from pot. Keep compost around root ball.

3. Wrap roots in damp sphagnum moss. Tie in place with plastic-coated wire.

4. Hold moss and plant on bark and bind in place with more wire.

5. When bark is in position check plant is upright. Spray regularly and make sure root ball does not dry out.

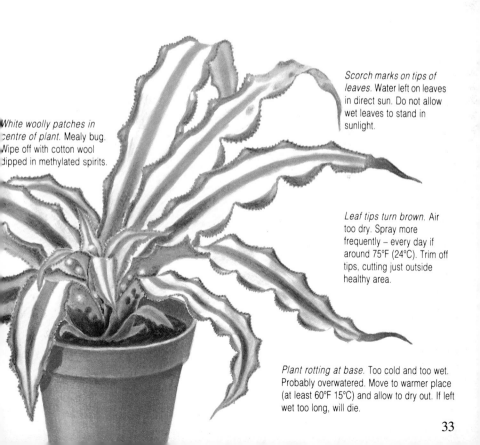

White woolly patches in centre of plant. Mealy bug. Wipe off with cotton wool dipped in methylated spirits.

Scorch marks on tips of leaves. Water left on leaves in direct sun. Do not allow wet leaves to stand in sunlight.

Leaf tips turn brown. Air too dry. Spray more frequently – every day if around 75°F (24°C). Trim off tips, cutting just outside healthy area.

Plant rotting at base. Too cold and too wet. Probably overwatered. Move to warmer place (at least 60°F 15°C) and allow to dry out. If left wet too long, will die.

33

Umbrella grass

This is a more unusual plant for the adventurous collector. Though it is not particularly difficult to grow, it benefits from careful attention as its stems bend and crease easily. It is a graceful and elegant plant, taking its common name from the way its green, slender leaves hang down from the top of its long stems. The stems of Umbrella grass grow to 39in (1m) tall, while those of a smaller variety, *Cyperus alternifolius*, are about half this length. Small brown flowers grow out from the centre of the top of the stem. Since this is really a bog plant, it likes plenty of water.

They can be divided in early spring if they are becoming very large. New plants can also be grown from flower heads. When flowers die, cut off the tips of the leaves on one stem and bend the stem so the leaves are submerged in a bowl of tepid water. Keep warm, changing water every 3–4 days and new plantlets will grow from the old leaf.

Light: Prefers a light position, but keep away from mid-day sun.
Temperature: Winter minimum 55°F (12°C). Summer up to 68–77°F (20–25°C), if well watered.
Water: Keep compost wet at all times; better if standing in water. Water every day in summer, and if in centrally heated rooms.
Humidity: Spray daily in summer, 3 times a week in winter.
Feeding: Every 14 days in the growing season (spring and summer) with house-plant food diluted according to the maker's instructions.
Soil: Loam-based No. 2 compost.
Repotting: Annually in spring, though prefers a pot slightly too small.
Cleaning: Humidity spraying sufficient. Soft summer rain good. No leafshine.

The stems of Umbrella grasses, topped by an elegant cluster of slender leaves, grow up to 39in (1m) tall. Small brown flowers appear in the centre in summer. Handle the plant with care as the stems easily bend and crease. Make sure new plants have no yellow leaves.

Leaves turn quickly yellow or brown. Needs water urgently. Soak in bucket of water for 10–15 minutes. Place on saucer to drain, and leave standing in water that soaks through. Spray regularly.

Cutting down stems
1. If plant dies down in winter, cut off stems with scissors just above soil level.
2. Keep pots standing in water and in spring, the stems will reshoot.

Plant does not grow or produce new leaves in summer. Feed every 7 days for about 3 weeks, then continue at 14 day intervals. Do not increase strength of food.

White insects on leaves which fly off when leaves touched. Whitefly. Spray every 14 days with derris or pyrethrum-based insecticide until clear.

what
goes
wrong

Leaves bleached. Too much sun. Move out of direct sunlight.

Leaves sticky and covered with small green insects. Edges of leaves nibbled. Greenfly. Spray every 14 days with pyrethrum or diluted malathion-based insecticide until clear.

Leaves look scorched. Leafshine damage. Do not use. Cut off damaged leaves.

Leaves look dull and limp. Too dark. Move to lighter place but not full sunlight.

Leaves die in winter. Too cold. Cut off withered foliage. It will reshoot in spring. Keep above 55°F (12°C).

Stem bent and damaged. Plant has been knocked. Stems crease easily so keep in a safe position. Cut off broken stem at soil level.

Dragon tree

This is one of many popular species of *Dracaena* and is tolerant of most room conditions. There are several varieties available, most grown with new foliage sprouting from canes from 12in (30cm) to 6ft 6in (2m) high. Adult plants produce an attractive scented flower spike with cream-coloured blossoms – but these are rarely seen indoors.

Dracaena fragrans is an all-green variety but there are others, such as *D. fragrans* 'Massangeana' that are variegated, with a broad yellowish stripe down the centre of the leaves. Plants growing on canes of different heights can be placed together to make an unusual display.

Most Dragon trees are grown from imported sections of stem from 12in (30cm) to 6 ft 6in (2m) long and around an inch (2½cm) across. When kept under glass by the growers, these sprout an elegant rosette of new leaves. When buying this type of plant, make sure that the cane is well rooted in the pot.

Light: Prefers good light position away from direct sunlight. Plain green varieties will tolerate more shade than variegated types.

Temperature: Winter minimum 60°F (15°C), though will tolerate 55°F (12°C) if water withheld. Summer maximum 75°F (24°C).

Water: Twice a week in summer, once a week in winter. Plant must neither stand in water nor completely dry out.

Humidity: Spray with tepid water 2–3 times a week.

Feeding: Every 14 days with liquid houseplant food diluted according to the maker's instructions.

Soil: Peat-based or loam-based No. 2 compost.

Repotting: In spring, every other year, for large plants. If too awkward to handle, just change topsoil.

Cleaning: By hand with damp cloth. Use leafshine sparingly once a month. Too much leafshine will clog the pores of the leaves.

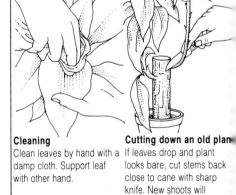

Cleaning
Clean leaves by hand with a damp cloth. Support leaf with other hand.

Cutting down an old plant
If leaves drop and plant looks bare, cut stems back close to cane with sharp knife. New shoots will appear.

Brown scorch marks on leaves. Too much direct sun. Move out of full sunlight. Do not spray in sunlight.

New leaves small and distorted or plant does not grow at all. Needs feeding. Feed every 14 days all the year round.

Greyish brown spots on leaves. Leaf spot fungus. Spray once with a systemic fungicide.

Stem rots from top. Too cold and draughty. Keep at temperature of at least 60°F (15°C). Move into protected position.

Leaves yellow with webs underneath. Red spider mite. Spray with derris, diluted malathion or systemic insecticide every 14 days until clear. Increase humidity by spraying daily.

Leaves discoloured with brown scales under leaves and on stems. Scale insect. Remove with cotton wool dipped in methylated spirits or spray with diluted malathion or systemic insecticide every 14 days until clear.

Plant flops, leaves turn yellow and rot; roots rot. Too wet, overwatered. Allow to dry out before watering again. Do not stand in water.

White woolly patches on leaves and stems. Mealy bug. Remove with cotton wool dipped in methylated spirits or spray with diluted malathion every 14 days.

Leaves fade. Too dark. Move to lighter position but not full sunlight.

Lower leaves droop and curl under, edges yellowing, tips brown. Needs water, may also be too hot. Water more frequently so that it never dries out. Check temperature and move to cooler place if possible. Spray daily to increase humidity. When old, the lower leaves may turn yellow and drop naturally.

what goes wrong

Bottom leaves drop. Caused by sudden changes in temperature, often on way from shop to home. New leaves will grow.

Plant sheds leaves and stops growing. Too cold. Move to warmer place, over 60°F (15°C).

37

Elettaria cardamomum

Cardamom plant

A member of the Ginger family, in its native land the Cardamom plant is grown commercially to produce a spice, cardamom, which is much used to flavour curries and other dishes. It makes a good indoor plant, growing to about 12in (30cm) in the house. Its shoots look rather like bamboo, and the oblong leaves grow at intervals of 1½in (4cm) up the stems. When touched, they give off an aroma reminiscent of cinnamon. The plant is not always easily available, but is worth searching for as its leaf formation and shape make a good variation on other houseplants. It occasionally produces small flowers. Its many stems grow from a thick underground rhizome and can be divided in spring if becoming overcrowded in pot.

The Cardamom plant's all-green leaves grow on stems that sprout from an underground rhizome. It survives well in poor light and cannot stand summer sun. Look for plants with several healthy stems and leaves with no brown tips or edges.

Light: A window that does not face the sun is best. Keep out of direct sunlight, especially in summer.
Temperature: Winter minimum 60°F (15°C), summer maximum 75°F (24°C). Likes good ventilation, especially in very hot weather.
Water: Twice a week in summer, once every 10 days in winter. If temperature drops to or below minimum, withhold water.
Humidity: Spray 3 times a week in summer, especially if hot, and once a week in winter.
Feeding: Every 14 days in the growing season (spring and summer) with houseplant food diluted according to the maker's instructions.
Soil: Loam-based No. 2 or peat-based compost.
Repotting: Annually in spring as plant starts to make new growth.
Cleaning: Humidity spraying sufficient. Use leafshine every 3–4 weeks.

Entire leaves turn brown. Needs watering, or kept in too hot and dry atmosphere. Water more often and move to cooler place if possible. Spray regularly. Remove brown leaf.

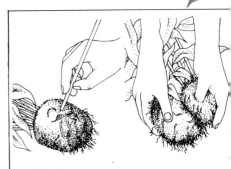

Root division
1. If pot is overcrowded with stems, in spring, remove plant from pot and gently tease stale soil from around roots and rhizomes.
2. Pull stems and roots apart, keeping a good portion of rhizome and root in each section. Repot each half in the normal way.

...o new leaves or shoots appear. Needs
...eeding or, if in spring, repotting. Examine
...ots to see if they are crowded.

Leaves look bleached. Too much direct sun.
Move out of full sunlight, especially in summer.

what
goes
wrong

...eaves flop. Too cold. Move
...warmer room, at least
...°F (15°C).

*Leaves look dull and lose
colour*. Too dark. Move to
lighter position but not full
sunlight.

...aves turn yellowish and
...ve webs underneath.
...d spider mite. Spray with
...uted malathion every 14
...ys until clear. Increase
...midity by spraying or
...anding pot on damp
...bbles.

Tips of leaves turn brown.
Air too dry. Increase humidity
by spraying or stand pot on
saucer of damp pebbles.
Edges may turn brown if too
cold.

*Brown scales and sticky
coating on stems and
under leaves*. Scale insect.
Remove with cotton wool
dipped in methylated spirits
or spray every 14 days with
a systemic insecticide until
clear.

...ant turns black and rots
...base. Too wet,
...erwatered. Allow to dry
...t before watering again,
...en water less often. But
...ay be fatal.

*Leaves have silvery scarred patches.
Black insects around plant*. Thrips.
Spray every 14 days with systemic
insecticide until clear.

39

Fatshedera lizei

Ivy tree

This interesting houseplant is a cross between a False castor oil plant *(Aralia japonica)* and an ivy. Its leaves are similar to those of the False castor oil plant, but smaller, and it has tiny rather uninteresting green flowers like an ivy. It grows upright (though its thin stems need to be supported with a cane or moss pole) and will climb like an ivy. Very tolerant of different room conditions, it is also quick growing and makes a good display when several plants are grown together up a moss pole.

The most common variety has all green leaves but there is a variegated type with slightly smaller leaves.

The Ivy tree's glossy five-pointed leaves grow from a thin stem which is best trained as a climber. Variegated plants have creamy white markings, usually at the leaf edges. Healthy plants will have leaves growing all down the stems with no yellowing foliage.

Light: Best in good light away from direct sunlight, but quite tolerant of shady conditions. Variegated plants need more light than all green ones.

Temperature: Winter minimum 45°F (8°C), summer maximum 65°F (18°C).

Water: 2–3 times a week in summer, so that only the top ½in (1cm) of soil dries out; every 7–10 days in winter so that it is drier but does not dry out completely.

Humidity: Spray 2–3 times a week when growing in spring and summer, once a week in winter. If temperature is higher than 65°F (18°C), a daily spray will help plant to survive.

Feeding: Every 14 days in the growing season (spring and summer) with houseplant food diluted according to the maker's instructions.

Soil: Loam-based No. 2 compost.

Repotting: Annually in spring, just as plant starts to grow. Put 3 plants together in a pot for a bushier effect.

Cleaning: Humidity spraying sufficient, though leaves can be cleaned with a damp cloth if they get dusty or dirty. Use leafshine every 2–3 months.

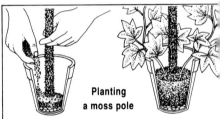

**Planting
a moss pole**

1. Prepare pot with drainage material and position moss pole in centre. Add compost to hold it upright.

2. Place plant roots on compost. If several are planted together, space them evenly around pole.

3. Add compost to fill pot, covering roots. Firm it around both roots and moss pole. Make sure pole stands upright.

4. Fasten plant stem to po with twine or raffia, tying loosely in space between leaves. Do not damage shoots.

what goes wrong

New shoots elongated with long spaces between leaves. Too dark. Move to lighter place.

White woolly patches on leaves and in leaf axils. Mealy bug. Remove with cotton wool dipped in methylated spirits or spray every 14 days with diluted malathion or systemic insecticide until clear.

Leaves turn soft and yellow. Too wet, overwatered. Allow to dry out before watering again, then water less often. Top ½in (1cm) of soil can dry out between waterings. In winter, water only every 7–10 days. Never stand in water.

Leaves distorted and sticky with small green insects underneath. Greenfly. Spray with derris, diluted malathion or a systemic insecticide every 14 days until clear. Increase humidity by spraying regularly.

Variegated plants turn all green. Too dark. Move to lighter place but not full sunlight.

Leaves look limp and dull. Too hot. Does not like temperatures over 65°F (18°C). Move to cool place if possible and spray regularly in hot weather.

Leaves flop. Needs water. Water immediately and then 2–3 times a week in summer, every 7–10 days in winter.

Grey mouldy patches on leaves. Botrytis (grey mould). Spray with systemic fungicide and move to warmer, more dry position. Do not overwater in winter.

Leaves yellow with webs underneath. Red spider mite. Spray with diluted malathion or systemic insecticide every 14 days until clear. Increase humidity by spraying, especially in hot weather. Keep cooler.

Plant collapses after repotting. Roots damaged. Place whole plant in polythene bag or damp newspaper for two days.

Weeping fig

This is the best-known of the small-leaved varieties of *Ficus*. Its branches droop gracefully, particularly as the plant reaches adult size, making it much favoured by interior designers. Its leaves are bright mid-green, growing to about 3in (8cm) long and 1in (2½cm) wide, with many on each stem. It needs a good, light position to flourish, but is susceptible to cold draughts in winter. If it sheds leaves because of the cold, it will usually recover if moved to a warmer place, but draughts can be fatal. There are several varieties of this *Ficus,* some of which have variegated leaves. In good conditions, the Weeping fig will grow into an elegant tree up to 15ft (5m) tall. Though in time its trunk becomes strong and woody, younger plants need to be supported.

Light: Needs plenty, but must be kept out of direct sunlight.

Temperature: Winter minimum 55–60°F (13–15°C), summer maximum 75°F (24°C).

Water: Not more than twice a week in summer, once every 7–10 days in winter, with tepid water. Must not be over-watered, nor should it stand in water. Rainwater ideal, as tap water may cause lime deposits on root system, slowing growth.

Humidity: Mist spray daily, except when temperature below 60°F (15°C).

Feeding: Every 14 days in the growing season (spring and summer) with houseplant food diluted according to the maker's instructions.

Soil: Loam-based No. 2 compost.

Repotting: Annually in spring when young; just change topsoil annually when too big to handle easily.

Cleaning: Humidity spraying sufficient. Use aerosol leafshine about once a month.

The Weeping fig's leathery, waxy leaves help it to be tolerant of dry air, though it does better with a daily mist spray to provide local humidity. Do not buy plants with bare stems near the base. Protect them from cold draughts on the way home.

Leaves dry and turn brittle. Too dry, air too dry and too hot. Water more often and spray every day to increase humidity. Try to keep below 75°F (24°C).

Tying to a cane
Young and medium-sized plants need to be supported by a strong bamboo cane, especially when being carried. Tie plant to cane loosely, between side branches.

what goes wrong

eaves drop when green. oo dark or in draught, or ere has been sudden drop temperature. In winter, ater used was too cold. heck care conditions and iove if necessary to warmer lighter place. May shed ome leaves naturally when ew ones grow in spring.

Leaves blacken. Leaf has touched cold window. Move away from glass.

Leaves discoloured with brown scales on stems and under leaves. Scale insect. Remove with cotton wool dipped in methylated spirits or spray every 14 days with systemic insecticide until clear.

Leaves yellow and speckled with webs underneath. Red spider mite. Spray with diluted malathion or systemic insecticide every 14 days until clear. Increase humidity by spraying, especially in hot weather.

Sooty mould on leaves. Follows attack by scale insect. Wipe leaves clean with soapy water.

spring new leaves are mall, plant looks dull and feless. Needs repotting if mall or topsoil changing. eed after changing topsoil ut not for 3–4 weeks if ompletely repotted.

Leaves turn yellow, then fall. Too wet, overwatered or standing in water. Drain any water from saucer and allow to dry out. Wait until soil feels dry and crumbly before watering again.

43

Ficus repens

Creeping fig

This useful and beautiful climbing plant, sometimes known as *F. pumila,* flourishes in humid and damp conditions. Though it is first cousin to the rubber plant, it does not look in any way like one, having thin trailing or climbing stems and a mass of small green leaves. The plant will grow quite fast in good conditions, and will climb up the wall of a conservatory or up a moss pole, producing trails of up to 18in (46cm) in a year. It also makes a good plant for mixed bowls, in hanging baskets and in bottle gardens. The variegated variety of the plant is a slow grower. Related to the Creeping fig and similar in growth pattern is *F. radicans,* the Rooting fig, which has larger, stiffer and often variegated leaves.

The Creeping fig's small heart-shaped leaves grow close together on thin stems, forming a mass of green. Healthy plants look bushy, with no bare stems or shrivelled leaves. In spring and summer there should be signs of strong new shoots.

Light: Does well in shady situations away from a window and may become dried up in direct sunlight.

Temperature: Winter minimum 45°F (8°C). Will stand a summer temperature as high as 82°F (27°C), provided good humidity is maintained.

Water: 2–3 times a week in summer, every other day in winter to keep damp at all times.

Humidity: Spray every day in summer (twice if over 75°F, 24°C), every other day in winter.

Feeding: Every 14 days in the growing season (spring and summer) with houseplant food diluted according to the maker's instructions.

Soil: Loam-based No. 2 or peat-based compost.

Repotting: Annually in spring if necessary, though best in small pot, i.e. when plant is pot-bound.

Cleaning: Humidity spraying sufficient. No leafshine.

Stems grow straggly with leaves spaced wide apart. Much too dark. Move to a lighter position, but not full sun.

Humidity

Spray every day in summer and every other day in winter or if in centrally heated room.

If temperature above about 75°F (24°C), stand pot on saucer of pebbles almost covered in water. Do not let pot base touch water.

New leaves stay small or plant does not grow in summer. Needs repotting. Use pot one size larger.

Leaves turn yellow and drop. Too wet, pot perhaps left standing in water. Pour away any water in saucer and do not water again until compost feels barely moist.

what goes wrong

White woolly patches on leaves. Mealy bug. Remove with cotton wool dipped in methylated spirits or spray with diluted malathion or systemic insecticide every 14 days until clear.

Leaves discoloured with brown scales. Scale insect. Remove with cotton wool dipped in methylated spirits or spray every 14 days with diluted malathion or systemic insecticide until clear.

Leaves yellow with webs underneath. Red spider mite. Spray every 14 days with derris, diluted malathion or systemic insecticide until clear. Spray daily to improve humidity.

Leaves dry up and curl. Too dry or too sunny. If compost feels dry soak plant in bucket of water for 10–15 minutes, then drain. Pick off dried leaves and water regularly. Keep out of direct sun. If all leaves dry out, plant will not recover.

Fittonia verschaffeltii

Painted net leaf

This attractive creeping plant with its spectacular leaf markings is not, perhaps, the easiest of plants to cultivate, but is most rewarding when growing well. It is a useful plant for shady positions away from direct light, but it needs warmth and high humidity. It is also a good plant for mixed bowls and for large bottle gardens or terrariums. A Painted net leaf has attractively patterned camellia-shaped leaves about 3–4in (8–10cm) long. The small green flower which appears in the summer should be removed from the plant so that all its growing strength goes into the leaves. The miniature silvery-marked form often seen is a related species, *Fittonia argyroneura*.

A healthy Painted net leaf is basically green, with distinct white veins, shaded in red. A miniature form with more silvery veins is known as the silver net leaf or snakeskin plant. Plants should be compact, with no curled or dropping leaves. Though difficult to keep for long in dry, centrally heated rooms, they are well worth the extra effort.

Light: Tolerates shade, and will deteriorate if put in direct light, even if not in sunlight.
Temperature: Minimum all the year round 65°F (18°C) as plant likes to be warm at all times. If temperature above 80°F (27°C) humidity should also be high.
Water: At least 3 times a week in summer, more if near 80°F (27°C), and about every 5 days in winter, as plant must never dry out. Check compost regularly and use soft water if possible.
Humidity: Spray daily in summer, every other day in winter, to maintain essential high humidity.
Feeding: Every 14 days, using houseplant food diluted with water. Use half as much food as the maker recommends.
Soil: Loam-based No. 2 or peat-based compost.
Repotting: Annually in spring into shallow or half pots if possible, as plant has shallow root system. Good drainage in pot essential.
Cleaning: Humidity spraying sufficient. No leafshine.

what goes wrong

Lower leaves turn yellow. Too wet, soil waterlogged. Check drainage holes in pot are not blocked and empty any water from saucer. Allow to dry until soil is just moist.

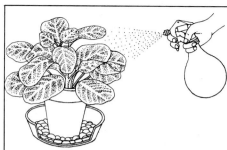

Humidity
Fittonias must be kept constantly humid. Spray every day in summer, every other day in winter.

If leaves turn dull and shrivel, stand pot in saucer on pebbles almost covered with water. Make sure pot base is not touching the water.

Leaves distorted and sticky with green insects. Greenfly. Spray with pyrethrum or a systemic insecticide every 14 days until clear.

New leaves small and spaced widely on stem. Too dark. Move to lighter place but not in a window.

Leaves go dull and shrivel at the edges. Air too dry. Spray every day and stand pot on saucer of damp pebbles, making sure that pot base is not in water.

Brown burn marks on leaves. Leafshine damage. Do not use.

Leaves shrivel, turn thin and papery. Too dry and/or too much light. Soak immediately in bucket of soft water for 10–15 minutes, then drain. Move to semi-shaded position. Remove leaves that do not recover and water more often.

Leaves drop and no new ones appear. Too cold. Move to warmer room, at least 65°F (18°C) and make sure it is out of any draughts.

Grevillea robusta

Silk oak

This interesting evergreen tree makes a good house or conservatory plant when young. It has large, bronzy-green, fern-like fonds which can be as long as 12in (30cm), and which are silky on the underneath side. It will stand quite low temperatures so is hardy in temperate climates, such as the south-west of England and frost-free areas of the U.S. It is easily grown from seed and, when young, is often mistaken for a fern. It grows rapidly, however, provided it is in a good light position, even in full sun which it prefers. In its native Australia it will grow up to 100ft (30m) high and indoors may reach 6ft (almost 2m) in three years. While small it looks good in mixed plantings but when it gets bigger is best on its own.

A healthy Silk oak has bronzy-green, fern-like foliage with a smooth, silky underside. It grows best in a sunny position but does not need high temperatures. Make sure plants look fresh and vigorous, with no dry or drooping leaves.

Light: Best in full sunlight.
Temperature: Winter minimum 45–50°F (8–10°C); normal room temperature in summer, though if over 70°F (21°C), air circulation must be good.
Water: Up to 3 times a week in summer, especially if over 70°F (21°C). Once a week in winter, withholding water altogether if very cold.
Humidity: Spray twice weekly during growing season in summer. About every 14 days in winter, unless 50°F (10°C) or below.
Feeding: Every 10 days in growing season (spring and summer) with liquid houseplant food diluted according to the maker's instructions.
Soil: Likes lime-free compost if possible but loam-based No. 2 is suitable.
Repotting: Annually in spring. If it is growing fast, use a new pot 2 sizes larger than the old. When it is too awkward and heavy to handle easily, change the topsoil only and start feeding again immediately.
Cleaning: Humidity spraying sufficient. No leafshine.

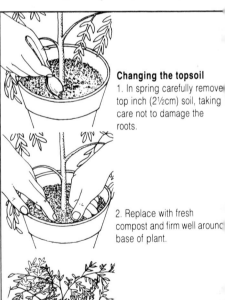

Changing the topsoil
1. In spring carefully remove top inch (2½cm) soil, taking care not to damage the roots.

2. Replace with fresh compost and firm well around base of plant.

3. Water well and add dose of liquid houseplant food to the water to give immediate nourishment.

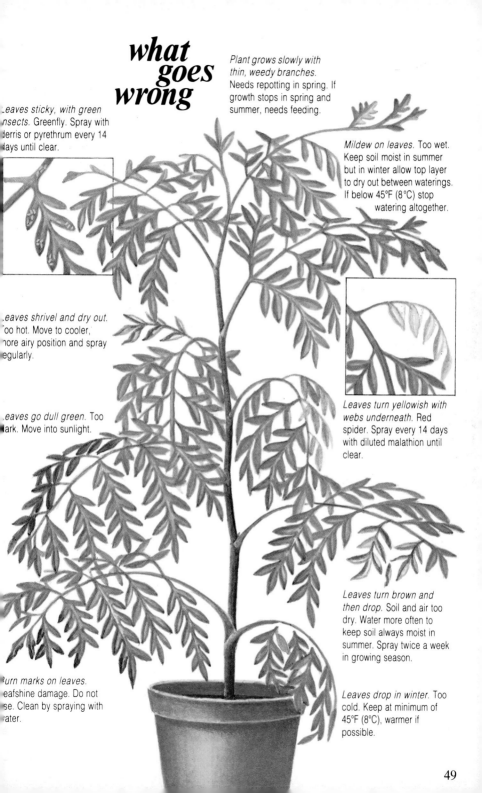

what goes wrong

Plant grows slowly with thin, weedy branches. Needs repotting in spring. If growth stops in spring and summer, needs feeding.

Leaves sticky, with green insects. Greenfly. Spray with derris or pyrethrum every 14 days until clear.

Mildew on leaves. Too wet. Keep soil moist in summer but in winter allow top layer to dry out between waterings. If below 45°F (8°C) stop watering altogether.

Leaves shrivel and dry out. Too hot. Move to cooler, more airy position and spray regularly.

Leaves go dull green. Too dark. Move into sunlight.

Leaves turn yellowish with webs underneath. Red spider. Spray every 14 days with diluted malathion until clear.

Leaves turn brown and then drop. Soil and air too dry. Water more often to keep soil always moist in summer. Spray twice a week in growing season.

Burn marks on leaves. Leafshine damage. Do not use. Clean by spraying with water.

Leaves drop in winter. Too cold. Keep at minimum of 45°F (8°C), warmer if possible.

Velvet plant

Looking not unlike a high-class nettle, this ornamental plant has distinctive purple, hair-covered leaves and stems. It produces small, unpleasant-smelling yellow flowers which should be removed, as they take strength away from the fast-growing leaves. The Velvet plant looks good as a young plant in mixed bowls where its colour contrasts well with green-leaved plants. It tends to become lanky when old, so it is wise to take cuttings and start new plants at least every two years. An easy plant to grow, it likes plenty of light. It can be kept bushy by pinching out the growing tips of straggly stems or can be grown as a trailer in a hanging basket, or trained round a hoop.

The Velvet plant's distinctive toothed leaves are covered with fine downy hairs and when healthy and kept in good light, have a rich purple colour. The flowers (which smell unpleasant) should be removed as they appear. New plants should be bushy with no sign of a flower spike.

Light: Grows well in full sunlight, which improves the purple colour of the leaves.
Temperature: Winter minimum 60°F (15°C), though will survive 55°F (13°C) if water withheld. Summer maximum 70°F (21°C).
Water: Every other day in summer, once a week in winter. Do not water if temperature falls to 55°F (13°C) or less. Shake surplus drops from leaves to avoid scorching by sun.
Humidity: Benefits from standing in saucer of pebbles almost covered in water, but this is not essential.
Feeding: Once a month in the growing season (spring and summer) with house-plant food diluted according to the maker's instructions.
Soil: Loam-based No. 2 compost.
Repotting: Repot at start of second year, when if not grown as a trailing plant in a hanging basket it may also need staking.
Cleaning: Spray once every 3–4 weeks on a dull day. May be dusted with small hair-brush. No leafshine.

Plant looks straggly with long spaces between leaves. Needs feeding or, if over 2 years, growing old. Take cuttings from healthy stem tips in spring.

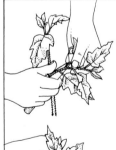

Preparing a stem-tip cutting
1. Cutt off tip of healthy stem, including 2 pairs of leaves and growing point. Trim off stem below a leaf.

2. Remove lowest pair of leaves so there is a section of bare stem. When planted lowest leaf should be just above compost. Keep mois and warm (65–70°F, 18–21°C) for 21 days. Cover with polythene bag to keep humid, removing it for 5 minutes a day.

what goes wrong

New leaves are small and a flower spike appears. Remove flowers so that growing strength goes into leaves.

Leaves distorted and sticky with green insects. Greenfly. Spray with pyrethrum or a systemic insecticide every 14 days until clear.

Leaves and stems wilt. Too dry. Soak in bucket of water for 5 minutes, then drain. If plant flops over and does not grow well but is correctly watered, may need repotting. Check roots to see if they are crowded in pot.

Burn marks on leaves though no water sprayed. Leafshine damage. Do not use.

Leaves lose purple colour and turn all green. Too dark. Move into sunny spot.

Leaves look scorched. Water left on leaves after watering or spraying. Shake surplus water off foliage. Do not spray in full sun.

Plant collapses and stems rot. Overwatered or too cold. Overwatering can kill. Allow plant to dry out before watering again and check drainage in pot. Keep above 60°F (15°C).

51

Hedera helix

Ivy

Ivy was one of the first plants to be grown in the home and is one of the few houseplants that are native to Europe. Indoor ivy is grown in many varieties with leaf sizes ranging from finger-nail size up to 2½in (6cm) across. Some are all green, others highly variegated. Ivies are very easy plants to keep and because of this are sometimes neglected. They do not like too hot or too dry an atmosphere and do best in the company of other plants. They make beautiful hanging basket plants and look good trained up to a trellis. If lower stems become bare and straggly nip out the leading shoots a couple of times a year to keep the plant bushy.

There are very many varieties of Ivy with leaves of different sizes, patterned in different shades of green and white or green and cream. Healthy plants should have bright, firm leaves and be compact with strong shoots growing from the centre.

Light: Best in good light, though direct sun can bleach the leaves. The greater the leaf variation, the more light needed.

Temperature: Winter minimum indoors 45°F (8°C). Best summer temperature 60–65°F (15–18°C); if temperature higher, increase humidity.

Water: Twice a week in summer, once a week in winter sufficient.

Humidity: Spray every day in summer or centrally heated rooms, once a week in cooler positions. To increase humidity, stand plant in saucer of damp pebbles.

Feeding: Every 14 days in the growing season (spring and summer) with houseplant food diluted according to the maker's instructions.

Soil: Loam-based No. 2 or peat-based compost.

Repotting: Annually in spring for mature (2 years and over) plants. Young, quick-growing ones may need repotting twice a year if they look too large for their pot. If very large, change the topsoil every year.

Cleaning: Humidity spraying sufficient, though if very dusty wipe with damp cloth. Use leafshine once a month.

Stems grow lanky with long spaces between leaves; leaves drop. Too cold and to dark. Move to lighter, warmer place, over 45°F (8°C).

Repotting

When roots grow out of pot base and plant stops growing, it needs repotting.

Remove from old pot and carefully tease soil from around root ball. Do not damage roots. Repot in pot one size larger, and leave without water for 2 days to encourage roots to spread through soil.

what goes wrong

Leaves discoloured with brown scales. Scale insect. Remove with cotton wool dipped in methylated spirits or spray every 14 days with pyrethrum or a systemic insecticide until clear.

Leaves turn pale in summer. Too much direct sun. Move to slightly shaded place.

Variegated plants turn plain green. Overfeeding or too dark. Check conditions and move to lighter place if necessary. Stop feeding until following spring.

Leaves turn yellow with webs underneath. Red spider mite. Spray with diluted malathion every 14 days until clear.

Silvery marks on leaves. Thrips. Spray with pyrethrum or a systemic insecticide every 14 days until clear.

Leaves turn black all over. Too wet, overwatered. Allow to dry out before watering again, then water less often. In winter let top half inch (1cm) of soil dry out between waterings.

Leaves go quite dry and crisp. Too hot and dry. Move to cooler room (under 65°F, 18°C) if possible. Spray daily to improve humidity.

Black sooty patches on leaves. Sooty mould. Wipe off with 6 or 7 drops of disinfectant mixed with a cup of water.

Leaves distorted and sticky with green insects. Greenfly. Spray every 14 days with pyrethrum or a systemic insecticide until clear.

53

Freckle face

This plant, grown essentially for its pretty coloured oblong leaves, which grow to 1½–2in (3–5cm), has recently been improved by careful breeding. Once a rather untidy, sprawling plant, it is now much more compact and makes a good ground cover plant for mixed planted bowls. Its distinct colouring also makes a good contrast to green or variegated plants. Though it can be overwintered, it is best propagated afresh each spring to keep it neat and compact. Older plants produce delicate purple and white flowers.

It can be propagated from either stem-tip cuttings or from seed. Both need a warm place (70°F, 21°C) and cuttings should be covered with polythene to provide extra humidity.

Light: Needs good light. A window that does not face into the sun is good. Leaves lose pink markings in too dark a position, but direct sunlight will burn them.

Temperature: Winter minimum 65°F (18°C), if possible. Ordinary room temperature adequate in summer. If very hot – over 75°F (24°C) – ensure plant is in an airy position.

Water: 3 times a week in summer, once a week in winter with tepid water, when not growing.

Humidity: Unless planted in mixed bowl, stand in saucer of pebbles almost covered with water. Do not spray.

Feeding: Every 14 days with liquid houseplant food diluted in water. Use half as much food as the maker recommends.

Soil: Loam-based No. 2 compost.

Repotting: Annually in spring if plants are being kept from year to year. It is better to repropagate each spring, to keep stock young, vigorous and compact.

Cleaning: Dust carefully with soft cloth. No leafshine.

If they are not kept in good light, the leaves of a Freckle face plant will lose their attractive pink markings. Bright sunlight, however, will burn them so if they are in a sunny window, make sure the light is filtered through a fine net curtain. Leaf markings vary from tiny pink dots to larger, more widely spaced patches, all on a green background.

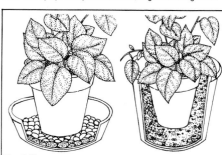

Humidity

Humidity is important all the year round. Spraying may damage the leaves so stand pot on saucer of pebbles almost covered in water. Don't let pot base touch the water or roots will become waterlogged.

Or pot can be placed in outer container with damp peat packed between.

Leaves lose their markings. Too dark. Move to lighter position in window but out of direct sun.

Burn marks on leaves. Direct. sun. Move away from sunny window. Or leafshine damage. Do not use.

Leaves droop and look dull. Too cold or water used too cold. Move to warmer place, over 65°F (18°C) and water in winter with tepid water.

Leaves turn yellow and drop off. Too wet, overwatered. Allow to dry out before watering again, then water less often. In winter once a week is sufficient, so that top half of soil dries out.

Leaves pale with brown scales. Scale insect. Remove with cotton wool dipped in methylated spirits or spray with systemic insecticide every 14 days until clear.

what goes wrong

Leaves curl inwards and go dry and papery. Too hot and dry. Place in cooler, more airy position (under 75°F, 24°C) and stand on saucer of damp pebbles to improve humidity. If soil dry, add water.

Musa cavendishii

Dwarf banana

While the Dwarf banana is easy to grow and is tolerant of most conditions, as long as it has plenty of moisture and good air circulation, it is not suitable for a small room as its long, graceful leaves can reach 39in (1m) when matured and are very delicate. They split easily along the veins if knocked or if the atmosphere is dry. When kept in good light and warm conditions, the plant will grow very quickly, making up to 39in (1m) in a year, and it will even give fruit if grown in a conservatory. Some varieties can be grown quite easily from seed.

Light: Best in light, sunny position.
Temperature: Winter minimum 60°F (15°C), normal room temperature in summer. Do not leave in closed up room in hot weather.
Water: 2 or 3 times a week in summer when growing, never allowing plant to dry out. Every 10 days sufficient in winter, when plant can be much drier. Never leave water on leaves, as this can cause scorch marks in sun.
Humidity: Spray every other day in summer, weekly in winter. Stand on saucer of wet pebbles to increase humidity.
Feeding: Every 14 days in the growing season (spring and summer) with house-plant food diluted according to the maker's instructions.
Soil: Rich loam-based No. 3 with a little manure added.
Repotting: Annually in spring. For plants that are too large to handle easily, replace topsoil.
Cleansing: Humidity spraying sufficient. If very dirty, wipe leaves carefully with soft cloth, supporting underneath to avoid damage. No leafshine.

The Dwarf's banana's leaves are up to 39in (1m) long when it is fully grown but are very delicate. They unfurl one by one from the plant's centre, gradually forming a trunk-like stem. Healthy plants have no brown edges to the leaves and should show no sign of splits or tears.

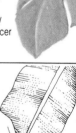

Leaves torn and damaged. The delicate leaves tear easily if knocked. Move to safe position. Dry air may cause leaves to split. Spray every other day in summer or in centrally heated room, and stand pot on saucer of damp pebbles.

Removing a damaged leaf
Cut leaf stem with sharp knife as close to the main stem as possible. Dust cut edge with sulphur dust to protect from infection. If sap runs, seal cut with vaseline.

Cleaning
If leaves are dusty, wipe them carefully with a soft cloth and sponge with tepid water. Support the delicate leaves while cleaning.

No sign of new leaves in spring. Needs repotting (or topsoil changing) and feeding. If replacing topsoil, feed immediately. If repotting, do not feed for 14 days.

eaves shrivel and go thin nd papery. Leaf edges may lso turn black and leaf radually die. Too cold. love to warmer place, at east 65°F (18°C) and remove ead leaves.

Burn marks on leaves. Leafshine damage or direct sun on leaves, especially after spraying. Do not use leafshine and do not spray plant in sunlight.

eaves turn pale. Too dark. love to lighter place. If in unny window, do not spray vhile sun is on leaves.

White woolly patches in leaf axils, especially older leaves. Mealy bug. Remove carefully with cotton wool dipped in methylated spirits or spray with diluted malathion every 14 days until clear.

Slimy rot on stems and base. Too wet or sprayed too often in low temperature. Dust rot with sulphur dust and move to warmer room, at least 65F (18C).

Webs under leaves, leaves discoloured. Red spider mite. Spray every 14 days with diluted malathion until clear.

Lower leaves turn yellow. This is natural in older leaves, which gradually die and fall.

what goes wrong

Leaf edges turn brown and leaves dry up. Too dry. Water more often and improve humidity by spraying every other day in summer or in central heating and standing pot on saucer of damp pebbles.

57

Pandanus veitchii

Screw pine

Described by an eminent Victorian botanist as a 'stately, fine-looking plant,' the screw pine needs plenty of room to be seen at its best, as it leaves may grow over 3ft (1m) long and spread out gracefully. They grow in a circle from the central stem which appears to twist as it ages, giving the plant the first part of its common name. The 'pine' comes from the leaves' resemblance to pineapple leaves. When the plant is 2–3 years old it develops aerial roots which grow down to the soil, raising the plant as if on stilts.

The Screw pine's sharp-edged leaves are green with creamy white or yellowish stripes near the edges. Growing in a spiral pattern from the centre, they arch down gracefully, making a striking display. They need good light and because of their spiked leaves should be kept in a place where they will not be accidentally touched.

Light: Likes plenty, except mid-day sun. Needs some sunlight every day and will deteriorate if in too dark a position.

Temperature: Winter minimum 50°F (10°C), though water must be withheld at this temperature and plant better kept at 60°F (15°C). Can be in normal room temperature in summer, though if very hot (75°F, 24°C or above), needs increased humidity and plenty of air.

Water: 2–3 times a week in summer, every 10 days with tepid water in winter, withholding altogether if temperature drops to winter minimum. At all times, ensure no water left in leaf axils as this can cause rotting. Best watered from below.

Humidity: Spray with tepid water once a week in summer, every 10–14 days at other times. Keep on saucer of damp pebbles.

Feeding: Every 20 days in the growing season (spring and summer) with houseplant food diluted according to the maker's instructions.

Soil: Loam-based No. 2 compost with peat added in proportion of 4:1.

Repotting: Usually every 12–15 months in spring, though plant best in small pot.

Cleaning: Wipe leaves with damp cloth, or use leafshine every 3 weeks.

Repotting

Repot in spring when roots are very crowded and new leaves are small. Water plant well first. Prepare pot one size larger with drainage layer and layer of damp, loam-based No. 2 compost mixed with peat.

1. Hold old pot with one hand over compost, around base of plant. Tap edge of pot and plant and old compost will come out.

2. Carefully tease away stale soil but do not damage the roots or aerial roots. Place plant in centre of new pot, resting root ball on compost. Cover roots with compost but leave about 1–2in (2½–5cm) space between top of compost and pot rim.

3. If aerial roots grow later in the year, cover them with fresh compost in autumn.

eaves turn all green,
lant does not grow. Too
ark. Move to lighter place.
lake sure plant is in morning
r afternoon sun.

eaves pale and bleached.
oo much midday sun. Plant
eeds morning or afternoon
un every day but not fierce
oonday light.

New leaves small.
Needs feeding or
repotting. Check roots to
see if they are very
crowded in pot and if
so, repot in next size of
pot.

Leaves shrivel and turn
brown. Too hot and dry.
Water more often and move
to cooler place (under 75°F,
24°C if possible).

rown scales and sticky
oating under leaves.
cale insect. Remove with
otton wool dipped in
ethylated spirits and spray
th diluted malathion every
4 days until clear.

Leaves rotting. Drops of
water left on leaves after
spraying or watering. Water
from below and if
temperature 50°F (10°C)
allow soil to dry out.

what goes wrong

Brown marks on edges of
leaves. Air too dry. Stand
pot on saucer of damp
pebbles to improve humidity.

ebs under leaves and
llow marks on surface.
d spider mite. Spray with
uted malathion or systemic
ecticide every 14 days
il clear.

Base of leaf rotting. Too
wet, overwatered. Allow soil
to dry out before watering
again. In winter allow top
half of soil to dry out between
waterings, and if
temperatures below 50°F
(10°C) do not water at all.
Stem rot may be fatal.

Leaves soft, brown and mushy. Much too
cold, frost damage. Cut out dead leaves at
base and move to warmer room, preferably
at least 60°F (15°C).

Philodendron bipinnatifidum

Upright philodendron

Philodendrons are some of the easiest plants to grow in the house and so can be recommended for a beginner. The upright or bush type is a very useful plant and will normally survive in quite a dark position. Though not as popular as the climbing varieties, it is well worth growing. It has thick, slightly fleshy leaves which grow to about 15in (35cm) across on 2ft (60cm) stems. Older plants may produce even larger leaves, so are best grown on their own. Stems which lean too far out over the edge of the pot can be tied to a cane. When inserting canes, take care not to damage the roots. Cuttings can sometimes be grown from the small shoots at the base of the leaf stems, but they are difficult to root.

Light: Prefers good light position away from direct sunlight. Will tolerate positions away from the window.
Temperature: Winter minimum 55°F (12°C). Up to 75°F (24°C) in summer, provided good humidity is maintained.
Water: Twice a week in summer while growing, once a week in winter. Do not allow plant to stand in water.
Humidity: Mist with tepid water twice a week all the year round.
Feeding: Every 14 days in the growing season (spring and summer) with houseplant food diluted according to the maker's instructions.
Soil: Loam-based No. 2 or peat-based compost with fertilizer of No. 2 strength included.
Repotting: Annually in spring until plant is in 7in (18cm) pot. Then just replace topsoil in pot each spring.
Cleaning: Use damp cloth, supporting leaf from underneath. Use leafshine not more than once every two months.

This type of upright Philodendron has leaves about 15in (35cm) across. Healthy leaves are bright, glossy green, with deep indentations around the edges so that they are split almost to the centre vein. Young leaves are scarcely indented at all but develop their characteristic shape as they grow older.

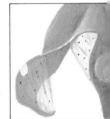

Webs under leaves, leaves start to discolour. Red spider mite. Spray with diluted malathion or systemic insecticide every 14 days until clear.

what goes wrong

Leaves look dull and do not grow in spring. Too cold. Move to warmer place, at least 55°F (12°C).

Stems grow long and floppy.
Too dark. Move to lighter
position but not full sun.
Need not be by window but
does need some light to
flourish.

Cleaning
Clean the leaves with a
damp sponge or cloth,
supporting them from
underneath. Use leafshine
but not more than once a month.

*Leaves droop. Too hot and
dry.* Soak plant in bucket of
water for 10–15 minutes,
then drain. Water more often
and keep in cooler place.

*Leaves turn yellow then
drop.* Too wet, overwatered.
Check drainage holes in pot
are clear and allow to dry
out before watering again. In
winter allow top layer of soil
to dry out between
waterings.

*Scorch marks on leaves.
Direct sunlight.* Do not spray
n sunlight and keep plant in
hadier position.

*New leaves stay small or
none appear.* Needs feeding
or repotting. Check roots
and repot in spring if
crowded together. Feed
regularly when growing.

61

Pilea cadierii

Aluminium plant

This attractive, compact plant is easy to grow and does well in mixed bowls with other types of plants. As it is inclined to become a little straggly, the young shoots should be picked out in mid-summer to make the lower stems grow more bushily. The leaves are oval in shape, measuring about 1½in long by ¾in wide (37mm x 18mm) and are dark green with silvery markings. They grow in pairs up the stems, with several stems sprouting together in one pot. There are several varieties of the plant including a miniature version, *P. cadierii nana* and *P. mollis* or 'Moon Valley' an exciting new one with crinkled leaves.

Light: Does well on windowsill out of direct mid-day sun. Tends to grow leggy if away from light. Leaves must not touch window glass in winter.

Temperature: Winter minimum 60°F (15°C), though survives at lower temperatures if water withheld. Summer maximum 70°F (21°C).

Water: 2–3 times a week in summer. Once a week in winter, though compost should never dry out.

Humidity: Spray daily in summer and about once a week in winter unless in very hot room (70°F, 21°C), when a daily spray will help. Shake off surplus water if plant in direct sunlight.

Feeding: Every 14 days when growing in spring and summer with liquid houseplant food diluted according to the maker's instructions.

Soil: 3 parts loam-based No. 2 mixed with 1 part peat.

Repotting: In spring. Prune back stems by half before repotting so that plant grows bushily again.

Cleaning: Humidity spraying sufficient. If very dirty or dusty, use small dry paintbrush. No leafshine.

Healthy Aluminium plants have clean, clearly marked leaves. In spring and summer they should have vigorous growing tips and should look neat and compact. New leaves are paler at first, developing their colour as they grow.

New leaves small. Needs feeding or repotting. If rootball is tangled with no soil clinging to roots, repot in spring with new compost.

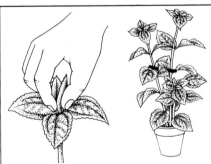

Pruning

If plant is growing straggly with more stem than leaf, pinch out growing tips. New shoots will grow from lower down the stem.

In spring, cut straggly plants back to half their height before repotting. Cut with scissors just above a pair of leaves.

lants grows straggly with long spaces between leaves. Too dark. Move to lighter place. Prune very raggly stems and pinch out growing tips to encourage bushy growth.

what goes wrong

hite woolly patches on leaves and stems. Mealy bug. Wipe off with cotton wool dipped in methylated spirits or spray with diluted malathion every 14 days until clear.

Leaves distorted and sticky with green insects. Greenfly. Spray with pyrethrum or systemic insecticide every days until clear.

Leaves droop. Needs water. Soak well in bucket of water 10–15 minutes, then drain. Water more often and spray regularly.

Plant collapses, all leaves and stems droop. Frosted, plant is dead.

Single leaf turns black in winter. Plant in window with leaf touching cold glass. Move away from window.

Patches of grey mould on leaves. Botrytis, caused by overwatering. Allow to dry out before watering again and dust affected leaves with sulphur dust.

Scorch marks on leaves. Leafshine. Do not use. Clean only by spraying or with a dry paintbrush. Pick off damaged leaves.

Leaves turn black and drop off. Too cold. Move to warmer room, at least 60°F (15°C).

Podocarpus macrophyllus

Indoor yew

This unusual houseplant grows into a tall tree in its natural environment but indoors is more shrubby and can be kept bushy by annual pruning. This variety comes from China and has flat, narrow leaves. Their undersides are bluish green and they grow on graceful side branches from the main stem. Indoor yews need good light at all times and do best in a sunny window. Otherwise they are not difficult to grow and do not require special care. Older plants may produce flowers rather like small catkins but these rarely appear indoors. Large plants need to be supported with a central cane.

Light: Requires full light at all times. Water must not be left on leaves in full sunlight.
Temperature: Winter minimum 45°F (7°C). Normal room temperature in summer; if very hot (75°F, 24°C or more), ensure plant is well-ventilated or put outside in its container.
Water: Twice a week in summer, once a week in winter to keep moderately moist at all times. Must not stand in water or become waterlogged.
Humidity: Spray 2–3 times weekly in summer, preferably in early morning; once a week in winter. Do not spray while sun is on the leaves.
Feeding: Every 14 days in spring and summer when growing with liquid houseplant food. Use half as much food as the maker recommends.
Soil: Loam-based No. 2 compost.
Repotting: Annually in spring when new growth starts. With large plants, just change topsoil in pot.
Cleaning: Humidity spraying sufficient. Use leafshine once a month.

The narrow leaves of the Indoor yew grow close together on their side branches. Healthy leaves have a bluish tinge underneath and are bright green on the upper surface. Choose plants that are bushy, with no bare stretches of s

Plant does not grow in spring and summer Needs feeding or repotting – or has been overfed. Check frequency and strength food; check roots. Do not repot unless the fill and crowd together in the pot.

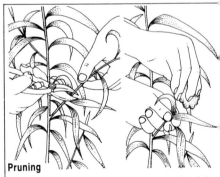

Pruning
To keep plants bushy and compact, prune side branches in spring or summer. Cut with secateurs just above a leaf.

Dust cut end with sulphur dust and if sap runs, seal end with vaseline.

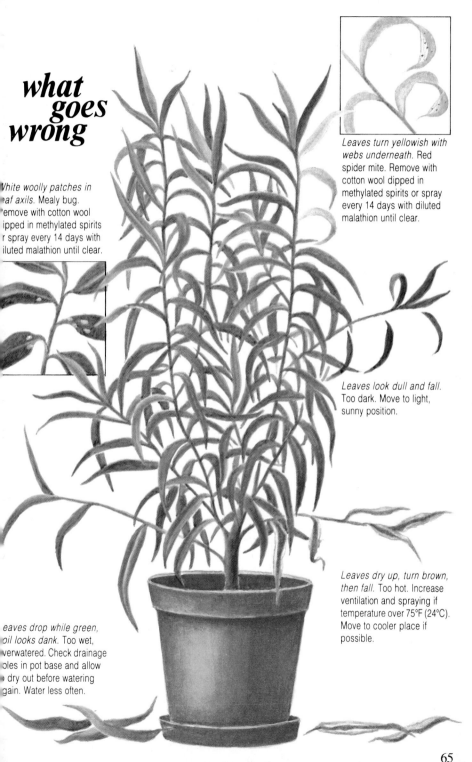

what goes wrong

White woolly patches in leaf axils. Mealy bug. Remove with cotton wool dipped in methylated spirits or spray every 14 days with diluted malathion until clear.

Leaves turn yellowish with webs underneath. Red spider mite. Remove with cotton wool dipped in methylated spirits or spray every 14 days with diluted malathion until clear.

Leaves look dull and fall. Too dark. Move to light, sunny position.

Leaves dry up, turn brown, then fall. Too hot. Increase ventilation and spraying if temperature over 75°F (24°C). Move to cooler place if possible.

Leaves drop while green, soil looks dank. Too wet, overwatered. Check drainage holes in pot base and allow to dry out before watering again. Water less often.

Grape ivy

One of the best climbing houseplants, this plant tolerates fairly shady positions and grow 2–3ft (60–100cm) a year. It makes a good room divider as it will cover a large area of trellis and also does well in a hanging basket when young. Older plants tend to develop woody stems which break easily under the weight of their hanging foliage. In mixed plantings, grape ivy should never be overwatered as plants growing together produce a humid microclimate of their own which protects them from drying out. Grape ivy is related to the true grape vine and climbs in the same way, with curling tendrils that attach themselves to a stake or trellis. It grows well in hydroculture.

Healthy Grape ivy leaves are dark, glossy green, about 2in (5cm) long with a series of small points around the edge. Young leaves may have a bronzy colour, which darkens to green as they grow. Plants should be well covered with leaves and have vigorous tendrils.

Light: Grows best by a window that does not face the sun but will survive in quite shady areas away from the window.

Temperature: Keep above 55°F (13°C) in winter and at normal room temperatures in summer.

Water: Usually twice a week in summer, every 14 days in winter. Do not overwater. Allow top layer of compost to dry out between waterings.

Humidity: Mist twice weekly in summer, same in winter if plant in hot, dry centrally-heated atmosphere. Stand pot in saucer of pebbles almost covered with water.

Feeding: Every 14 days in the growing season (spring and summer) with houseplant food diluted according to the maker's instructions.

Soil: Loam-based No. 2 compost.

Repotting: At least every spring. If growing well may require potting again in mid-summer. Change the topsoil of large pots or tubs in spring.

Cleaning: Humidity spraying sufficient. Monthly spray with leafshine beneficial.

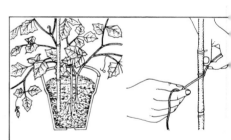

Tying to a cane

1. Push cane into compost a few inches from main stem until it is ⅔ down the pot.

2. Tie 9in (23cm) length of string to cane with knot on side next to stem.

3. Loop around stem between leaves.

4. Tie knot firmly against cane but do not crush stem with string.

Leaves drop and plant becomes straggly. Too dark. Move to lighter place but not in direct sunlight.

Young leaves distorted and sticky with green insects. Greenfly. Spray every 14 days with pyrethrum or derris until clear.

Leaves turn yellow and have webs underneath. Red spider mite. Spray every 14 days with diluted malathion or systemic insecticide until clear.

what goes wrong

Leaves turn pale and bleached. Too much sunlight. Move away from window that gets direct sun.

Young leaves stay small and pale. Needs feeding. Feed every 14 days while growing. If roots are showing through pot base, repot.

White woolly patches on leaves and stems. Mealy bug. Spray with diluted malathion every 14 days until clear or remove with cotton wool dipped in methylated spirits.

Leaves turn brown at tips. Scorched by sun. Move out of bright sunlight.

Leaves dry up, go thin and papery and drop. Too dry or too hot. Water more often and spray to increase humidity. Keep under 70°F (21°C) if possible.

Leaves look dull, droop and drop off. Too wet, overwatered. Allow to dry out, then water less often. Check drainage in pot is good and let top ½in (1cm) of soil dry out between waterings. Also caused by dry air. Spray to increase humidity in hot weather.

67

Sansevieria hahnii

Mother-in-law's tongue

This is a low-growing variety of the more familiar tall-leaved Mother-in-law's tongue. The leaves are short and stubby, growing in a formal rosette shape. The most common type has dark green leaves with slight mottling, but there is a variegated one which has a band of yellow on the outside edges of the leaves. Both are extremely slow growing. When mature, it will produce a flower spike with small yellow flowers. This should be removed when the flowers fade.

Like the taller variety, this plant is easy to grow as long as it is never over-watered. If planted in mixed bowls, where the shape and texture of its leaves contrast well with other house-plants, it should be kept in its own pot (see p. 69). It is also good grown on its own in places where space is a problem.

This variety of Mother-in-law's tongue has short, stubby leaves with pointed tips. Attractively mottled in shades of green, they grow in a rosette shape from the centre of the plant. Healthy leaves should have no brown marks or scars. They can be kept clean and shiny by wiping with a damp cloth

Light: Prefers full sunlight, which gives good colour to the leaves. Will survive in quite shady places.

Temperature: Winter minimum 50°F (10°C), if water withheld, otherwise 60°F (15°C) better. Summer maximum 75°F (24°C).

Water: Every 7–10 days in summer, 14–21 in winter, depending on heating. If in mixed bowls, keep in own pot and water separately.

Humidity: Don't spray. Prefers dry air.

Feeding: Every 21 days when growing in summer with houseplant food diluted with water. Use half as much food as the maker recommends.

Soil: Loam-based No. 2 compost.

Repotting: Every 2 years, as it grows better if pot-bound. Make sure roots well firmed in.

Cleaning: Wipe with damp cloth once a week. No leafshine.

Leaves pale and lose markings. Too dark. Move to lighter place, in full sunlight if possible.

Brown patches on leaves. Watered too often. Allow to dry out between waterings. Remove badly affected leaves at base with sharp knife.

what goes wrong

Leaves rot at base. Overwatering. Allow dry out before watering again, then water less often. Spots of rot on main part of lea caused by spraying. Do not spray. Remov damaged leaves at base with sharp knife.

Planting a mixed bowl

Because of their different water requirements, Sansevierias must be isolated from other plants in mixed bowls or troughs.

1. Put plant and pot in outer container with dry sand between the two.

2. Place this in mixed trough, hiding the rim with compost. It can now be watered separately.

3. When spraying the other plants, protect the Sansevieria with newspaper so that water does not get on its leaves.

Leaves dry up and turn brown. Too dry – probably quite dried out. May die but soak pot in bucket of water for 10–15 minutes, then drain well.

New leaves distorted with small insects. Vine weevils. Spray with pyrethrum every 4 days until clear.

Spots on leaves. Leafshine damage. Do not use. Clean by wiping with damp cloth.

White woolly patches on leaves. Mealy bug. Remove with cotton wool dipped in methylated spirits or spray with diluted malathion every 14 days until clear.

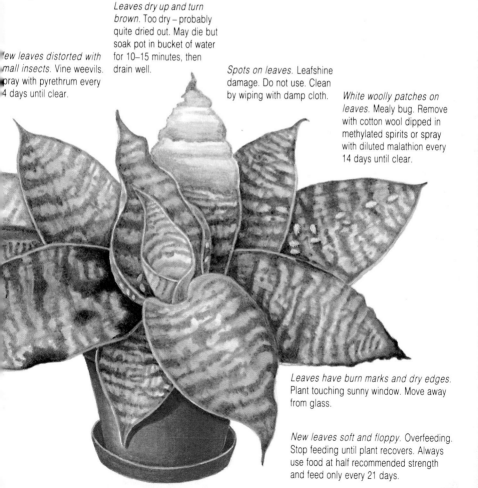

Leaves have burn marks and dry edges. Plant touching sunny window. Move away from glass.

New leaves soft and floppy. Overfeeding. Stop feeding until plant recovers. Always use food at half recommended strength and feed only every 21 days.

69

Saxifraga sarmentosa

Mother of thousands

Saxifragas are usually thought of as alpine plants, hugging a rocky scree covered in snow and ice in winter. They are therefore an unusual family of plants for the house, though this variety makes a good indoor plant. In summer it produces dainty white flowers and a mass of young plantlets grow on runners, slender stems which hang over the sides of the pot. If grown in a hanging basket, the runners and plantlets hang down attractively, while in a large bowl or trough, the plant will spread to cover a wide area. The leaves are green with lighter green or white vein markings and are slightly hairy. There is a variegated version with smaller leaves which needs a slightly higher minimum temperature.

Light: Windowsill shielded from hot summer sun ideal.

Temperature: Winter minimum 45°F (8°C), summer ideal 55–60°C (12–15°C), as plant prefers cool temperatures. Does not like hot central heating and may dry up in 70°F (20°C).

Water: 3 times a week in summer. In winter allow to dry out between waterings. Every 10–14 days probably enough unless rooms are very warm (70°F, 20°C). Test compost regularly. Good drainage is essential to prevent rot. Make sure that plants in hanging baskets are watered regularly as they dry out quickly in summer.

Humidity: Not important, provided temperature moderate. A fortnightly spray keeps foliage fresh in hot weather.

Feeding: Once a month in summer with houseplant food diluted with water. Use half as much food as the maker recommends.

Soil: Loam-based No. 2 compost.

Repotting: Annually in spring.

Cleaning: Spray with water if dusty or dirty. No leafshine.

The Mother-of-thousands, sometimes called the Strawberry plant because its runners are like those of the garden strawberry, has dark green leaves with lighter green markings along the veins. A fortnightly mist spray with water will keep them clean and dust-free.

what goes wrong

Leaves pale and dull. Too dark. Move to lighter place but shield from hot summer sun. Pale, brownish leaves also caused by hot direct sunlight.

Leaves distorted and sticky with green insects. Greenfly. Spray with pyrethrum or systemic insecticide every 14 days until clear. Plant is very susceptible.

White woolly patches on leaves and stems. Mealy bug. Remove with cotton wool dipped in methylated spirits or spray with diluted malathion every 14 days until clear.

Plant collapses, leaves limp, stems rot. Too wet, overwatered. Allow soil to dry out before watering again. Check drainage and water less often.

Plant flops. Too dry. Soak in bowl of water for half an hour, then drain well. Water more regularly.

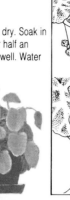

Propagation

1. Prepare small pot with drainage material and compost of ½ sand, ½ loam-based No. 2. Place next to parent plant and position plantlet in centre. Firm compost round it and water well.

2. When plantlet grows new leaves, sever runner close to new plant.

Burn marks on leaves. Leafshine damage, or direct sun. Do not use leafshine and move out of sunlight.

Stems grow straggly and leaves do not group together closely. Too hot (over 70°F, 21°C). Move to cooler place.

Webs under leaves, leaves begin to discolour. Red spider mite. Spray with diluted malathion every 14 days until clear. If temperature high (68–70°F, 18–21°C) spray every week to improve humidity.

Grey mould on leaves around base; leaves turn brown and shrivel. Botrytis, plant too wet and humid. Move to warmer place (55–60°F, 12–15°C) and allow to dry out before watering. Spray with systemic fungicide.

No runners or new leaves in spring and summer. Needs feeding. Feed every month in summer.

Leaves look ragged and many die. Old age. Propagate new plants from runners and throw old one away.

71

Syngonium vellozianum

Goose foot plant

This handsome climber is a little more demanding than other climbing plants and needs a humid atmosphere to grow well. It produces 6 or 7 new leaves a year, making around 12in (30cm) of new growth and supports itself by producing aerial roots which cling on to whatever the plant is climbing. It needs to be supported as it climbs and a moss-covered pole or a thin cane are both suitable. It can also trail from hanging baskets. The easiest variety has all green leaves; variegated plants grow more slowly and need good light to keep the patterning of their leaves. All-green plants do well in shadier places, out of direct sun. It is a good plant to grow in hydroculture.

Light: Keep out of direct sunlight. Tolerates shaded positions, especially the plain green varieties.

Temperature: Winter minimum 60°F (15°C). Optimum summer temperature 65–70° (18–21°).

Water: 3 times a week in summer with tepid water. Once a week in winter, also with tepid water. Allow the top layer of compost to dry out between waterings in winter.

Humidity: Spray daily. Stand pot in saucer of pebbles almost covered with water, but do not allow base of pot to touch water.

Feeding: Every 21 days in spring and summer when growing, with liquid houseplant food diluted with water. Use half as much food as the maker recommends.

Soil: 4 parts loam-based No. 2 compost to 1 part extra peat.

Repotting: Annually in spring. If growing fast so that roots show through pot base by midsummer, repot a second time.

Cleaning: Humidity spraying sufficient. If leaves get dusty or dirty, wipe with damp cloth. No leafshine.

Goose foot plants may have either plain green leaves or leaves patterned in green and creamy white. The variegated ones are slightly more delicate than the all-green ones and grow more slowly. Healthy plants should have plenty of bright, unmarked leaves and be firmly tied to a cane or moss pole.

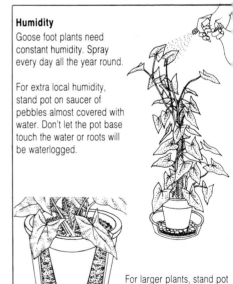

Humidity
Goose foot plants need constant humidity. Spray every day all the year round.

For extra local humidity, stand pot on saucer of pebbles almost covered with water. Don't let the pot base touch the water or roots will be waterlogged.

For larger plants, stand pot in outer container packed with damp peat.

Leaves turn pale with webs underneath. Red spider mite. Spray every 14 days with diluted malathion until clear. Plant is very susceptible. Spray with water daily and increase humidity by standing pot in saucer of damp pebbles.

what goes wrong

Stems grow straggly with long spaces between the leaves. Too dark. Move to lighter place but not full sunlight.

Plant droops and leaves look dull, curl and turn brown at edges. Stems rot at top. Too cold and wet, or in a draught. Move to warmer, draught-free place and allow to dry out before watering again. Water only once a week in winter.

Leaves turn brown and brittle. Too hot and dry, air too dry. Water more often and increase humidity by spraying and standing pot on saucer of damp pebbles. Move to cooler place if possible (under 70°F, 21°C). Cut off dead leaves.

Leaves look bleached. Too much direct sunlight. Move out of sun, into shadier position.

Leaves so pale they are almost transparent. Needs feeding. Feed regularly when growing, but use only half strength food.

Tetrastigma voinieranum

Chestnut vine

This vigorous climber can almost be seen growing, particularly in a warm, humid atmosphere, and it needs a lot of room. In ideal conditions, it may grow up to 6ft (almost 2m) in a year. If you have the space for it, it is an easy plant to keep, though it must not be over-watered. Young stems must be supported as they snap off easily if touched and look as if they can barely support their own weight. If a section of stem falls off, however, it does not seem to matter; the plant continues to grow and may even produce a new stem from the broken end.

Light: Prefers semi-shade in summer, full light in winter. As it cannot be easily moved, summer shade must be provided artificially, with a fine net curtain for example.

Temperature: Winter minimum 50–60°F (10–15°C), but enjoys high temperatures in summer provided humidity is good.

Water: Not more than twice a week in summer. It's best to let plant dry out between waterings. Keep on the dry side in winter, watering every 10 days, less if temperature drops to winter minimum (50°F, 10°C).

Humidity: Spray twice weekly in summer, once every 14 days in winter.

Feeding: Every 10 days when growing, in spring and summer, using liquid house-plant food. Dilute according to maker's instructions.

Soil: Loam-based No. 3 or peat-based with fertilizer added at No. 3 strength (see p. 10).

Repotting: Annually when young (up to 2/3 years), then just change the topsoil in spring.

Cleaning: Humidity spraying sufficient. If leaves get dusty, flick gently with a feather duster. Take care not to damage young stems. No leafshine.

Chestnut vine leaves grow in groups of four or five. Young leaves and new leading stems are covered with reddish brown hairs, while older leaves are dark green with a slightly matt finish. The curling tendrils attach themselves to the plant's supporting cane or moss pole.

what goes wrong

Burn marks on leaves, though plant not in sunlight. Leafshine damage. Do not use. Leaves look naturally matt.

Watering
Chestnut vines are susceptible to overwatering. Test compost before adding water to make sure it is dry below the surface. If still damp, do not add water. Never allow water to stay in the saucer for more than 10 minutes after watering, and make sure drainage holes in pot are kept clear.

74

Leading stems on new leaves small and brittle. Needs repotting or, if large, topsoil changing with fresh soil and fertilizer.

Plant flops. Too dry. Soak pot in bucket of water for 10–15 minutes, then drain. Water more often.

Leaves dry and curl up. Too hot and/or air too dry. Move to cooler place and increase humidity by spraying or standing pot on damp pebbles.

Leaves pale and bleached, with scorch marks. Too much direct sun in summer. Shade from sunlight.

White woolly patches on leaves and in leaf axils. Mealy bug. Remove with cotton wool dipped in methylated spirits or spray every 14 days with diluted malathion until clear.

Leaves pale, webs underneath. Red spider mite. Spray every 14 days with diluted malathion until clear. Increase humidity by spraying with water or standing pot on damp pebbles.

Leaves turn yellow, especially on older stems. Needs feeding. Feed every 10 days while growing.

Leaves fall. Too dark. Move to lighter place, full light in winter, filtered in summer.

Leaves droop and flop on stem. Too cold. Move to warmer place (at least 50–60°F, 10–15°C).

Stem and bottom leaves rot. Too wet, overwatered. Allow to dry out before watering again and water less often. Surface of soil should feel dry and crumbly between waterings.

75

Tolmeia menziesii

Piggy-back plant

Piggy-back plants get their common name from the way new plantlets grow on top of older leaves in spring and summer. The plantlets sprout from the point where the leaf joins its stem and if not removed, give the leaf a 'layered' look. The heavier leaves hang down over the edge of the pot and make this an ideal plant for a hanging basket. When well grown, they can produce almost a curtain of green. New plants may be easily propagated from the young plantlets, either by cutting off the parent leaf and standing its stalk in water, or in a mixture of moist sand and peat moss.

Light: Very tolerant of most conditions, although it can be burned by strong sunlight through glass. Plants kept in shady places will have paler leaves.

Temperature: Winter minimum as low as 33°F (5°C) provided water is withheld but ideally not less than 50°F (10°C). Plant prefers not to be too hot and stuffy in summer, so should be out of direct sun if temperature over 75°F (24°C).

Water: About twice a week in summer, once a week in winter, to allow top layer of compost to dry slightly between waterings. Use tepid water in winter.

Humidity: Stand pot in saucer of pebbles almost covered in water, especially if over 75°F (24°C). Never let pot base touch water or roots will be waterlogged.

Feeding: Every 14 days in spring and summer when growing with liquid house-plant food. Use half as much food as the maker recommends.

Soil: Loam-based No. 2 compost.

Repotting: Annually in spring, taking care not to damage runners carrying plantlets.

Cleaning: Occasional spray with water, about once every 14 days sufficient. No leaf-shine.

The leaves and stalks of the Piggy-back plant are covered with soft hairs. In spring and summer, small plantlets grow on top of the older leaves and can be used to propagate new plants. Healthy plants have well coloured green leaves growing close together at the centre, with new plantlets forming on some of the outer ones.

Leaves turn brown and curl. Too hot. Move to cooler place, less than 75°F (24°C) if possible. In summer, stand outside.

Dark brown burn marks on leaves. Leafshine damage. Do not use.

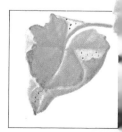

Leaves curl with webs underneath. Red spider mite. Spray with diluted malathion every 14 days until clear.

Propagation

1. In spring or summer, prepare small pot with drainage layer and compost made of half peat moss, half sharp sand.

2. Choose leaf with healthy plantlet attached and cut whole leaf off, with 1in (2½cm) stalk.*

3. Make small hole in compost with stick or pencil

and insert leaf stalk. Leaf with plantlet should lie closely on soil surface. Firm soil around stalk.

4. Water well. Keep soil moist but not saturated, with

pot in good light. In 2–3 weeks, plantlet will grow new leaves. About 6 weeks later, repot in loam-based No. 2 compost. Do not remove parent leaf until it is quite dried up.

what goes wrong

New leaves stay small and plant does not grow well or produce plantlets. Needs feeding or repotting. Check roots are not crowded in pot. Feed every 14 days in spring and summer.

Scorch marks on leaves. Direct sun through glass. Move out of hot summer sun.

Leaves and stems rot in winter. Too cold and wet; or water used too cold. Move to warmer place, at least 50°F (10°C) and do not water again until soil feels dry. Use tepid water in winter.

Crawling insects on compost and edge of pot. Earwigs. They damage roots. Dust with derris or pyrethrum every 14 days until clear.

Wandering Jew

This is one of the oldest, best-known and easiest to grow of houseplants. There are many varieties with a wide range of colours and growth habits. In most varieties, the oval, pointed leaves are multi-coloured, and if green leaves appear, they should be removed. Some varieties have small fluffy pinkish/purple flowers. They make ideal subjects for a hanging basket and are also a good ground cover plant for a mixed bowl or trough. As they tend to become a bit leggy when over a year old, it is best to repropagate each year. Cuttings 1½in–2in (3–4cm) long put 5 to a pot will soon root and grow to form a compact new plant. They can also be rooted in water. Cover a jar of water with kitchen foil and insert cuttings through small holes. Repot when roots form.

The leaves of this *Tradescantia fluminensis* 'Quicksilver' are attractively striped in green and white. Other varieties may be green with yellow, grey or even a pretty pink tinge. Trandescantias are such easy plants to keep that they are sometimes neglected. Healthy plants should be compact, with leaves growing to the bottom of their stems and no dried or discoloured patches.

Light: Tolerates fairly dark position; becomes leggy and variegations tend to revert to all-green if too dark.

Temperature: Winter minimum 50°F (10°C). Normal room temperature in summer, or put out-of-doors.

Water: Twice a week in summer, once a week in winter. Tolerates a little neglect.

Humidity: Spray every 14 days. Stand on saucer of pebbles almost covered with water but do not let pot base touch water or roots will be waterlogged.

Feeding: Every 14 days in the growing season (spring and summer) with liquid houseplant food diluted according to the maker's instructions.

Soil: Loam-based No. 2 or peat-based with fertilizer at No. 2 strength added (see p. 10).

Repotting: Best to repropagate in spring into 3in (8cm) pots. Then repot in early summer into 4in (11cm) pots.

Cleaning: Mist spray every 14–21 days with tepid water. No leafshine.

Leaves turn brown, shrivel and wilt; edges yellow or brown. Air too dry. Spray with water more often to increase humidity and stand pot on saucer of damp pebbles.

Leaves very pale with scorch marks. Too much direct sunlight. Move to position out of direct sun.

Propagation
To start new plants from old, straggly stems, cut stem tip including at least two pairs of leaves and growing tip, just below a leaf. Remove lowest pair of leaves to give enough bare stem to plant and insert in small pot of new compost. Keep moist and new leaves will soon start to grow.

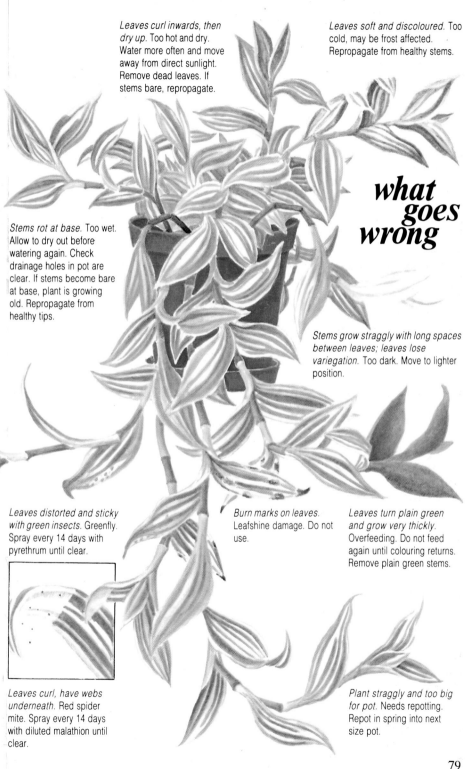

Leaves curl inwards, then dry up. Too hot and dry. Water more often and move away from direct sunlight. Remove dead leaves. If stems bare, repropagate.

Leaves soft and discoloured. Too cold, may be frost affected. Repropagate from healthy stems.

what goes wrong

Stems rot at base. Too wet. Allow to dry out before watering again. Check drainage holes in pot are clear. If stems become bare at base, plant is growing old. Repropagate from healthy tips.

Stems grow straggly with long spaces between leaves; leaves lose variegation. Too dark. Move to lighter position.

Leaves distorted and sticky with green insects. Greenfly. Spray every 14 days with pyrethrum until clear.

Burn marks on leaves. Leafshine damage. Do not use.

Leaves turn plain green and grow very thickly. Overfeeding. Do not feed again until colouring returns. Remove plain green stems.

Leaves curl, have webs underneath. Red spider mite. Spray every 14 days with diluted malathion until clear.

Plant straggly and too big for pot. Needs repotting. Repot in spring into next size pot.

Buying your houseplant

Florists, garden centres and specialist shops are best for unusual plants, large specimens and planted arrangements. Supermarkets, stores and service stations often offer excellent value in popular plants and rely on fast turnover to maintain quality. Market stalls may appear to offer good value but take care, especially in winter, when cold may affect the plants badly.

It is important before buying to consider where the plant is to go. Think about the room conditions, the light, heat or draughts that the plant may be subjected to. If you are a beginner choose a plant that is simple to grow. Don't be tempted to buy one that is exotic until you have had some experience.

Look carefully at the one you intend to buy. It should be firm in its pot, which should be clean. The compost on top should be fresh, not sprouting weeds or moss. None of the leaves should be marked, torn, yellow or faded. Beware of small plants in large pots; this probably means that they have just been repotted and the roots will not have grown properly into the fresh compost.

Always insist, particularly in winter, that the plant you buy is properly wrapped up, if necessary with a double layer of paper. Large plants often require support, with an extra cane to protect the growing tip. Take care not to knock it on the way home.

Lastly, make sure you know the plant's correct name so that you can look up its care instructions when you get home. Common names vary from place to place; the scientific name is the most reliable to use for identification.

Acknowledgements

Colour artwork by Andrew Riley/The Garden Studio
Line artwork by Marion Neville (pp. 1–5), Norman Bancroft-Hunt (pp. 6–13), Andrew MacDonald (pp. 14–78)
Photographs by David Cockroft
Plants by courtesy of Thomas Rochford & Son Ltd, Longmans Florists and the Royal Botanic Gardens, Kew
Additional photographs supplied by the Iris Hardwick Library of Photographs
Designed by Marion Neville
Typeset by Faz Graphics